THE COMFORTABLE
LIE

By

AC Williams

Published by Adriane Williams

3000 Whitney Ave

Ste# 211

Hamden, CT 06518

Cover design by Adriane Williams

ISBN 9798330462568

Printed in the United States

For my friend, my husband.

The piercing wail of sirens cut through the rain-soaked night as Detective Garcia pulled up to the cul-de-sac, his car's windshield wipers working overtime. A small crowd had already gathered, their faces sober under the flashing lights of the ambulance and police cruisers. Yellow crime scene tape stretched across the street, holding them back from drawing closer.

Garcia stepped out of his car, pulling his collar tight against the downpour, swore. He hated calls like this—senseless tragedies that shattered families and left too many questions unanswered. After years on the force, he had grown accustomed to seeing the aftermath of such disasters, but the weight of grief always hung heavy in the air.

An officer quickly radioed for a detective when it became clear they were dealing with a vehicular homicide. Detective Garcia surveyed the dimly lit street, his jacket soaked through, and rain dripping steadily off his hat. "Uh, Sarge, it was a hit-and-run," a young officer reported as Garcia approached. "Time of death: 3:15 a.m., Sunday, April 5th, 1989."

Garcia nodded grimly, his gaze shifting to a woman huddled in a fuzzy blue robe, trembling in the arms of a neighbor. Her soaked hair clung to her face, and she shook with uncontrollable sobs. The neighbor murmured comforting words, but it was clear the woman was beyond reach, consumed by her pain.

"I'll take her statement," Garcia said, bracing himself for what was always the hardest part of his job. As he knelt beside the woman, her tear-filled eyes locked with his, overflowing with wild, unrelenting anguish. "I... did the dishes …and… and. I was just taking out the trash," she choked out, her voice breaking. The detective gently patted Lillian's shoulder. He encouraged her to take her time. "And I heard a noise, so I checked the other side of the house. My daughter…, was still sleeping. Oh God!" She doubled over, her sobs overtaking her again.

'Garcia's voice was soft but steady. "Miss, I understand. You don't need to explain anymore. I have everything I need. Your son followed you out… that's all. It's not your fault." The words felt empty, but he said them anyway, knowing nothing could truly ease her pain.

However, a few miles away, a different scene was playing out. The drunk driver who had taken that little boy's life sat slumped in his car, blood trickled down his face. He was unaware of the blood, torn pajamas and debris stuck to the undercarriage. The car was lodged against a tree in his front yard, its hood crumpled like a piece of discarded paper. His head lolled against the window, the look on his face, serene. No way of knowing that beneath his car, blood and scraps of a child's pajamas were tangled with grass.

Chapter TWO

The morning sun streamed through the window, casting a warm glow on Tianna's room. Yet, a sense of melancholy lingered in the air. She thought back to her conversation with her bestie, a pang of worry tugging at her heart. Janiyah, once a vibrant and carefree spirit, seemed lost in a fog of indecision. Her relationship with Will had taken a toll on her, draining her of her money and usual spark. Tianna couldn't bear to see her friend suffer, but she also knew that she couldn't force her to make the right choices.

"Please don't sit on my bed with your street clothes," Tianna said, narrowing her eyes at her best friend, Janiyah.

Janiyah sighed dramatically, rolling her eyes as she settled onto the edge of a chair instead. "When did you become such a neat freak?" she asked, sucking on a lemon wedge.

Tianna gave her a teasing smile, though the firmness in her tone was clear. "My room, my rules."

The two had been best friends since sixth grade, surviving all the drama, boyfriends, and college exams that life had thrown their way. Janiyah and her parents moved to Brockton from Indiana. When their parents met they had slowly formed a friendship. people called them peanut butter and marshmallow fluff. But Janiyah was cool but lately

Janiyah couldn't help but notice how much Tianna had changed. Something in her demeanor was different—more guarded, more deliberate.

"Seriously, when did you turn into this uptight version of yourself?" Janiyah asked, feigning offense. Her playful tone carried a hint of genuine curiosity.

Tianna smirked. "It's called growing up. You should try it sometime."

Janiyah huffed, crossing her arms. "Growing up is overrated."

They both shared a brief laugh, though the tension lingered in the air. Janiyah bit her lip before admitting, "Will called me again. Says he's changed, but I don't know if I believe him."

At the mention of Will, the lightness in Tianna's voice faded. She rolled her eyes. "Why are you even thinking about giving him another chance?" she asked, her voice firm but not harsh. "You deserve better than being someone's convenience."

Tianna sighed, rolling over to check her phone. A notification from social media caught her eye, a photo of Will with another girl, laughing and cozy. Her friend was unaware, at that moment, William was not hugged up with his 'Bae Janiyah' but someone else, again. And it was not the right time to mention it. Janiyah was pouring out her undying love. A wave of anger washed over her. How could she still be blinded by his empty promises?

Janiyah shifted uncomfortably. “We’ve been together for three years, Tee. It’s not that easy to just walk away.”

“It doesn’t matter how long you’ve been with him,” Tianna replied. “What matters is how he treats you, and it’s not like you’re happy.”

Janiyah let out a frustrated sigh, her shoulders slumping. “I know, but sometimes I wonder if this is the best I’m going to get.”

Tianna softened, placing a hand on Janiyah’s arm. “Don’t talk like that. You’re smart, you’re beautiful, and you have so much to offer. Don’t let him make you doubt that.”

"Janiyah's bravado faltered for a moment as she met Tianna's gaze, a sad smile playing on her lips. 'Thanks, Tee. You have been confident since I met you. I wish I could see myself the way you do.' Tianna squeezed her arm reassuringly. 'You will. Just promise me, you'll stop giving him so many chances.' Janiyah nodded, her resolve wavering. 'I'll try,' she replied, though they both knew it would be easier said than done."

Back in Brockton her mother just returned home, and her husband was in the garage working on his car. Lillian put down her groceries massaging the day frustrations out of her shoulders. The table was set and fixed their plates. Slippered feet under the table met work boots and in five minutes the fork clattered to the plate. He was done eating, Lillian's food still warm, she continued eating. With a look her left at the rooster wall clock, she was sure, he would stay out until 3 am

Chapter THREE

As Tianna checked the clock, she stood up abruptly. "I've gotta head out soon. I'm meeting some friends from my psych class to talk about a radio segment we're doing next semester." Janiyah's eyes widened in surprise. "Look at you, Miss 'I-don't-have-time-for-anything-but-studying,' going on the radio now?"

Tianna pretended that it was not a big deal, but couldn't hide her excitement. "It's just a small thing, but I'm actually looking forward to it. Maybe giving advice on-air will be easier than doing it in person." Janiyah grinned. "Just don't turn into one of those self-righteous 'Dear Abby' types."

"I'll try my best," Tianna said with a laugh. "But seriously, think about what I said. You're worth more than waiting for Will to grow up." Janiyah gave her a weak smile as Tianna grabbed her bag and headed for the door. "I'll see you later," she called out.

"And, Tee? Good luck with your radio thing," Janiyah added. "I know you'll crush it."

Tianna smiled, a small wave of relief washing over her. As she walked out the door, she felt hopeful—not just about the radio show, but about the chance to help her best friend see her own worth.

The day stretched ahead of Tianna with the promise of new opportunities, yet she couldn't shake the thought of Janiyah. She knew she couldn't control her friend's choices, but she hoped Janiyah would eventually realize what she truly deserved.

After the podcast recording wrapped up, Tianna found herself lingering in the empty studio, her classmates' voices fading into the distance as they filed out. She glanced at the equipment, her mind still buzzing from their conversation about "Struggle Love." The term had sounded almost ridiculous at first, but as the discussion deepened, it became painfully clear how many people lived through it—how love could be a constant tug-of-war, full of sacrifices and wounds that never seemed to heal.

She thought about her own family—how her parents had been caught in that kind of struggle for as long as she could remember. A brief flash of her mother's face crossed her mind, Lillian's eyes always distant, clouded with grief and secrets. Tianna pushed the thought aside, trying to focus on the excitement of being back at school, but it was no use. The past had a way of creeping in when she least expected it.

As she packed up her things, her phone buzzed with a text from her father, Ralph. It was a simple message, asking how she was doing, but even that stirred something inside her—something uneasy. Tianna's fingers hovered over the screen as she considered what to write back, but she decided to leave it for later.

The familiar feeling of being torn between two worlds settled in again. Here at school, everything seemed manageable, almost easy. But back home, there was always a shadow—a sense that something was unresolved, something deeper than just family drama. Richie. Her brother's name echoed in her mind, a reminder of the tragedy that still clung to them all.

She shook her head, pushing the memories aside for now. She wasn't ready to deal with that—not yet. Instead, she gathered her things and headed out of the studio, ready to immerse herself in the normalcy of college life. But as she walked through the quiet campus, her thoughts remained back in Brockton, with her mother, wondering how Lillian was spending her evening.

Lillian was still at work, her mind elsewhere as she shuffled papers at her desk. The office had been her escape for years—a place where she could bury herself in tasks and forget the silence waiting for her at home. Each day, it was the same: she stayed late, finding any excuse to prolong her time at the office, yet knowing full well that no amount of work would fill the void left in her heart.

By the time she finally packed up and headed home, the streetlights had already flickered on, casting soft glows over the quiet neighborhood. Lillian unlocked the front door to her house, stepping inside to a familiar emptiness that greeted her like an old friend. The walls were quiet, the air still. It had been years since the sounds of children's laughter filled these rooms.

After dropping her keys on the counter, Lillian moved to the kitchen, where she began preparing dinner. The rhythm of chopping vegetables and stirring pots brought a strange sense of comfort—something to focus on, something to keep her mind from wandering too far into the past. But as she passed the hallway, her eyes inevitably drifted toward the closed door of Richie's old room. Even after all these years, she still wasn't ready to face it fully. Most of his things had been given away long ago—his toys, his clothes—but there were a few precious items she couldn't part with. A small collection of his favorite things remained, tucked away in the closet.

Her hand paused on the edge of the counter, and for a moment, she stood frozen, staring at the door. It had been so long since she last stepped inside, yet the memory of his laughter still echoed in her mind. She exhaled slowly, her heart tightening as she reminded herself that it was time—time to let go of what little remained of him in this house.

But it wasn't easy. She had tried before—more than once—but every time she went to pack up the last of his toys or his tiny clothes, something stopped her. Some days, she would pick up one of his old shirts, pressing it to her face, hoping to catch even the faintest hint of him. The scent had faded long ago, but the memories never did. She then turned back to the stove, Lillian told herself again that this time would be different. She would clear out the room, donate the last of his things, and move on. But as the weight of the house pressed in around her, she knew it would never be that simple.

She crossed the room slowly, her eyes landing on the small box of toys she hadn't been able to part with. Kneeling beside it, she picked up a small, worn-out teddy bear—one of Richie's favorites. She pressed it gently to her nose, even though she knew the scent was gone. A tear slipped down her cheek as she whispered to the empty room, "It's been years, baby. It's time." But still, she couldn't bring herself to let the items go.

Chapter FOUR

Lillian stood at the kitchen sink, her hands submerged in soapy water, the late afternoon sun streaming through the window. By now they were pruny. I may need moisturizer, she mumbled out loud. She then stared out into the yard where her children played, their laughter ringing through the air. For a brief moment, it was as if the weight of her grief lifted, and she was transported back to a time when life felt simple and whole.

"Mom! Watch me!" Richie, her youngest, shouted with glee. She looked up just in time to see him leap off the swing set, landing with a triumphant grin on his face. He was a bundle of energy, his small frame barely managing the jump, but his pride was undeniable. Lillian's heart swelled as she wiped her hands on a dishtowel, savoring the joy in her son's smile.

Richie's laughter echoed, blending with the shouts of his sister, Tianna, who cheered him on from the sidelines. Lillian allowed herself to believe, just for a moment, that everything was as it used to be—before life had become tangled in sorrow and unspoken pain. She cherished these moments, but they were tainted by a shadow she could never shake. Beneath her smile was the gnawing guilt—the guilt that weighed her down, night after night. She had failed him. Richie's death had been her fault. She had looked away for just a moment, just long enough for a tragedy to unfold.

The memory of that day haunted her, replaying in her mind like a never-ending nightmare. It wasn't just the accident itself; it was her actions that had led up to it. The distraction of her strained marriage, the emotional turmoil of following Ralph as he betrayed her again and again, had pulled her attention away when it mattered most. She had followed him that night, suspecting his infidelity, instead of staying home with her son. Richie had followed her, unseen, unnoticed until it was too late.

Years ago, this home had been filled with so much love. She remembered those warm summer evenings when she and her husband, Ralph, would dance in the living room. She'd twirl around in her dress while he held her close, whispering promises of a future they would build together. Their laughter had filled the space between them, a melody of hope and shared dreams. But that laughter seemed like a lifetime ago. Since Richie's tragic death, everything had changed. What once felt like a fairytale had soured into a constant struggle. The light that Ralph used to bring into her life dimmed, replaced by his late nights at work, his distant eyes, and the way he slipped through their home like a shadow, disconnected and unreachable.

"Mom, come on! You have to see this!" Richie's voice snapped her back to the present. Lillian forced a smile, holding onto the joy in his eyes for as long as she could. “I’m coming!” she called out, stepping into the yard.

Tianna, now a teenager, was beside Richie, encouraging him with a look that mirrored the same fire Lillian once had in her own eyes. The sight made Lillian's heart ache—seeing her daughter so full of life, yet knowing that Richie would never get the chance to grow up like his sister.

She watched them both, her emotions a mix of nostalgia and a longing that things could have been different. The yard, now overgrown in places where Richie used to run, seemed to echo with the ghosts of their past happiness. As the evening drew on, Lillian turned back to her daily routine, preparing dinner in the small kitchen that still smelled faintly of spices and memories.

She stirred the pot absentmindedly, her thoughts drifting back to Ralph. She recalled the way he used to smile at her, the way he’d make her feel like the most important person in the world. But those days felt like faded photographs—beautiful but blurry, distorted by the years of disappointment that followed. Ralph walked in later that night, the sound of the front door creaking open like a warning bell. He looked tired, worn out, and yet there was still that hint of defiance in his eyes. Lillian turned to face him, forcing a smile as he tossed his keys onto the table.

“Hey,” he said, his voice rough, a hint of forced casualness in his tone.

‘Hey,” Lillian answered back.

“What’s for dinner?”

They ate at the table in silence. It was a temporary truce. Her husband’s long legs stretched out almost coming in contact with hers underneath. That was the closest they had been in years. Later that evening, as Lillian cleaned up the kitchen alone, she found herself staring at the bottle of wine she had left untouched on the counter. Taking the corkscrew, she opened it, living with an alcoholic she did not know why she brought it in the first place.

Lillian imitated what she had seen others do, she really did not drink at all. She poured herself a glass, the liquid catching the dim light as she contemplated the choices that had led her here—to this point in her life where dreams of a happy marriage had turned to ashes. Lillian breathed in the aroma, swished the glass around before tasting it. With a deep sigh, she pushed back the memories, forcing herself to focus on the present. She knew that holding onto the past wouldn’t help her or her children. She had to be strong, for Tianna's sake, if not for herself. The front door creaked open again, and this time, it was Ralph standing there, a gust of cold northern air blowing in with him. He looked at Lillian, his expression blank, almost as if he didn’t recognize her.

“Lillian, we need to talk,” he said finally, his voice low and unsteady. He was drunk again, she thought. Biting her lower lip in deep thought, what was it this time. She turned to face him, her grip tightening on the edge of the counter. “About what, Ralph?” she asked, the calmness in her voice betraying the storm that raged inside her.

“About us. About everything that’s gone wrong,” he said, he wanted a cigarette, a drink, anything, but settled for his wife’s undivided attention. “I don’t know how to fix this.” The word divorce implied but left unsaid that time hung in the air the last time they argued.

Ralph opened his mouth as if to respond but then closed it, looking lost for words. For once, he didn’t have a quick retort or a deflecting joke. He just stood there, staring at the floor, the distance between them growing wider with every passing second. Maybe he was tired of cheating, she was sure as hell tired of being cheated on. It was time that they were free to do whatever they wanted. It wasn’t like Lillian did not know that the man she once loved was gone, replaced by the hollow shell of someone she barely recognized. And as she turned back to her children’s laughter echoing faintly from the yard, she realized that the only way forward was to stop trying to mend what was irreparably broken and to focus on building something new for herself and their remaining child.

That night, after trying to squeeze information out of Tianna before bed, Lillian sat alone in Richie’s old room. The silence was deafening. She let the tears she’d been holding back finally fall, mourning not just the loss of her son but also the life she had once imagined for her family. She knew the road ahead wouldn't be easy, but she also knew that she had to keep moving, even if it meant leaving behind the dreams that had once held her together. Lillian wished that Ralph died instead of her son. But there he remained soaked in self-pity, soaked in bourbon sitting on the floor speechless with tears rolling down his face.

Chapter FIVE

Tianna had barely settled back on campus after her summer break when she felt the familiar rush of excitement. Returning to Massachusetts University as a junior, she was determined to make her mark. Her hard work had paid off, and now, with her grades solid and her future plans in place, Tianna felt ready to take on the world. She had come a long way from her high school days, and she was more focused than ever on her goals.

"Ready for our first podcast?" one of her classmates asked as they set up equipment in the small studio. The topic for today was "Struggle Love"—the idea of being addicted to high-drama, emotionally taxing relationships. Tianna blinked in surprise. "Wait, what? Do people actually romanticize that?" she asked, shaking her head.

"I thought we were past the era of suffering in silence for love." But 'struggle Love' was in. But Tianna wanted to know why it was popular. One of the girls in the group shrugged. "You'd be surprised. A lot of people think being in love means dealing with the ups and downs, even if those downs are toxic." Tianna felt a surge of determination. She had grown up seeing the impact of "Struggle Love" in her own community, watching people settle for less because they thought it was all they deserved. This wasn't just a conversation for her; it was personal. Her mother briefly crossed her mind. But she failed to make the comparison. Even after all the family woes her father was the best person she knew.

"I think people get stuck in those relationships because they don't see their own worth," Tianna said, her voice steady. "They think the drama is normal, but it's not. Love shouldn't make you feel small or worthless."

The others nodded, and for a moment, the studio was quiet. Tianna knew she'd struck a chord. She was no longer the shy girl who hid behind books in high school; she was stepping into her role as a voice of reason, someone who could guide others away from the mistakes she'd seen so many people make.

`After the podcast wrapped up, Tianna made her way back to her dorm room. She was proud of herself but couldn't shake the underlying anxiety about going home for the next break. The thought of returning to Brockton filled her with mixed emotions. She loved her family, but the memories tied to that town were complicated, tangled up with the grief of losing her brother Richie and the strained relationship with her mother, Lillian.

Tianna packed her suitcase, she thought back to her last summer at home. Despite the comfort of familiarity, there was always a tension between her and her mother. Lillian was so strict, so controlling, always expecting more from Tianna. Her father, on the other hand, treated her like a princess—his "can-do" girl, as he always called her. Lillian put extra responsibilities on her and called her 'Can Do' as well but it held a different meaning.

When she finally arrived home, the familiar creak of the old wooden door seemed to echo with all the unresolved feelings she carried. "Heyyy….., I'm home!" she called out, her voice a mix of excitement and dread.

"Hi, darlin," Her dad called from the living room, slipping her forty dollars with a conspiratorial wink. "Want to grab some pizza? Don't tell your mother. Tianna grinned at him, feeling like a little girl again. "Sure, Dad. Let's do it," she said, pocketing the money. She knew her mother would be in the kitchen, probably cooking up a storm for her homecoming, but right now, she just wanted to be with her dad, away from Lillian's watchful eyes. As they backed out of the driveway, Lillian's voice trailed from the house, "Don't be gone too long! Dinner's almost ready! Tianna, come help me and tell me how everything is going at school. But within minutes Ralph was already backing out of the driveway.

Tianna rolled her eyes slightly, giving her dad a look that said it all. He just shrugged and smiled. He knew how to handle Lillian's nagging in a way that Tianna envied. To her, Lillian was like a storm that never cleared, always clouding over her happiness with questions and criticisms.

Later that night, after they'd eaten pizza and shared a few laughs, Tianna walked into the house to find her mother standing by the kitchen table, disappointment etched on her face. The food she'd prepared sat untouched, neatly packed away.

"You couldn't wait for dinner?" Lillian said, trying to keep her voice even.

"I told you I was making her favorites. I started as soon as I put my bag down and changed my clothes."

"We were just too hungry, Mom," Tianna replied, feeling a pang of guilt but not enough to apologize. "It's no big deal."

Lillian gave a tight smile, her eyes betraying the hurt she tried to mask. "I made all your favorites," she said softly. "It's fine, I'll save it for tomorrow." This was not about taking Tianna for pizza, this was about yet another affair.

This was Ralph's response to the argument they had just before Tianna arrived home. He was cheating again, and Lillian could not quite recall the name of the woman involved; it was something like Hope or Holly, she should have been named after a garden tool. This woman had even called their house once, seemingly it someone who had no emotional ties to Tianna's husband. Lillian laughed how convenient it was for both of them. Momentarily she was jealous of that freedom.

Tianna felt adrift, not knowing what the argument had entailed or how to respond, so she simply nodded, suddenly feeling as if she were back in high school, struggling to interpret her mother's mood swings.

As she made her way to her room, a lingering unease settled in her heart; no matter how much she accomplished, she felt she would always fall short in Lillian's eyes.

As the weeks passed, Tianna endeavored to enjoy her break, but her mother's incessant hovering and thinly veiled criticisms gradually took a toll on her spirit. One evening, after yet another fraught discussion concerning her career aspirations, Tianna finally reached her breaking point. "Why can't you just let me live my life without criticizing every decision I make?" she exclaimed, the frustration spilling out uncontrollably. Lillian's countenance fell, and for an unexpected moment, Tianna caught a glimpse of something more profound—vulnerability. "I just want what's best for you," Lillian replied quietly, her voice tinged with sincerity. "I don't want you to repeat the same mistakes I made. Finishing college…" But before she finished speaking Tianna cut her off.

"Mom, I will finish, and I am not even dating anybody!"

Having a child is like walking around with your heart muscle exposed, vulnerable to every injury. Lillian wanted her to be wiser than she was. Her daughter did not know or understand that her mother's criticisms stemmed not from a desire to control but from a deep-seated fear of her daughter suffering the same disappointments and unfulfilled dreams Lillian experienced. It was quiet again.

The rest of the evening passed in a rare and fragile peace, the kind neither Tianna nor her mother dared disturb. For the first time in years, the tension between them seemed to lift, leaving the air lighter, freer. Tianna allowed herself a small, cautious hope—maybe they were finally learning how to meet each other halfway.

As her break drew to a close, Tianna found herself eager to return to campus. Her upcoming radio segment awaited her, buzzing in her mind like a distant drumbeat of excitement. She packed her bags with an unusual sense of calm, and though the lingering unease of unresolved issues remained, she felt it was manageable now. This time, as she said goodbye to home, it was with less dread and a touch more understanding.

As she said goodbye to home, it was with less dread and a touch more understanding. Her thoughts wandered as she drove, her gaze catching the dimming light on the horizon. Gregory Stevens, a new hire at work, surfaced in her mind—unbidden but persistent. Running into him at the pizza shop had been unexpected, yet he'd left an impression she couldn't shake. There was something about his presence—solid, steady, almost grounding in its simplicity. Though she hadn't given much thought to dating, if she ever did, someone like Gregory seemed like the kind of person she could trust. The thought was fleeting, almost silly, but it lingered in the quiet spaces of her mind as the miles ticked by.

Gregory's life hadn't been simple, she knew that much. He'd grown up carrying more weight than most people his age. His father had left when Gregory was just three years old, slipping out the door without a word and never looking back. Gregory had spent years wondering if it had been his fault, if something about him wasn't enough to make his father stay.

His mother had carried her own quiet burden of guilt, though she never let it show. Women usually *did* bear the pressure when men left home. But his mother was a soldier. Instead of a pity party, she threw herself into raising Gregory, working long hours, yet finding moments to pour her wisdom and strength into her son. She refused to let the stigma of being a single mother define her, and to Gregory, she was a beacon of resilience. Where others saw struggle, he saw a woman who refused to break under the weight of life.

That strength had shaped him in ways Tianna couldn't help but admire. Gregory didn't wear his pain like a badge, nor did he let it define him. He simply endured, quietly and with grace.

By the time Tianna reached the familiar streets of campus, the thought of Gregory still clung to her, faint but persistent. Maybe it was his quiet strength that stirred something in her, or maybe it was the way he carried his past without letting it consume him. Whatever it was, it left her curious—about him, about what she might be looking for in someone, and about the parts of her life she hadn't yet explored.

True to his word, her father purchased her a small pull-a-part car to get around in, her mother kept complaining about being on a "fixed income." Most of its parts came from the junkyard, why was she complaining? But Tianna did not want to hear that, besides she could make it home and school in half the time. The city hummed with life as Tianna pulled into the lot, ready to dive back into her world. But for the first time in a long while, she felt a pull to something outside of it—a spark, faint but undeniable.

Back home Gregory's mother, striving to raise him to be the man his father wasn't, had been secretly saving. It is something big she would tell him. Gregory had no idea but knew she had everything under control. The stigma of being a single mother never affected her; she was never a stereotype to him.

He worked his way out of Brockton with a series of odd jobs—first at the pizza shop, where the hours were long but the pay was minimal, then later as a part-time mechanic's apprentice and delivery guy. He had started working young, just old enough to be trusted with an apron and the cash register. His mother had pulled double shifts at the hospital, and though he never said it, Gregory felt the weight of her exhaustion like a boulder on his chest. Every time she came home, her uniform wrinkled, shoes in hand, Gregory would watch the way her shoulders slumped forward. He promised himself he'd help any way he could. Anything to lighten her load.

Sometimes, he tried to remember what his father looked like, but the memories were blurry, like trying to see someone's reflection in a foggy mirror. His mother never talked about him either, and Gregory never asked. In many ways, he was fine with that. After all, his mother was the one who stayed. She was the responsible one. That was enough.

But there were moments when his father's absence burned into him—a flicker of frustration, a fleeting question of why his mother had to shoulder the burden alone. Why did he have to step up at such a young age? And why his father failed in showing up. Even as a teenager, there was a dull ache of resentment that sat in his chest whenever he saw other boys walking home with their fathers, laughing, arguing, playing catch. His classmates didn't understand what it meant to be the "man of the house" before you even became a man. Still,

Gregory never let those feelings show. He worked, and he worked hard. First at the pizza shop, where he earned enough to cover his own lunch money and occasionally slip his mother twenty bucks when he knew she was behind on bills.

Then he took up an apprenticeship at a mechanic shop, where he got his hands dirty, but the pay was better, and the hours allowed him to be home when his mother finally collapsed into bed after her shifts. She was a CNA back then, doing the grunt work at the hospital things nurses did not have to do, split-ups, bedpans and at times tending to patients who didn't even remember her name half the time. Gregory knew she hated the job, but she never complained. She told him that it was a stepping stone—she was saving up to become a registered nurse. "I'm working towards something better, Greg," she would say when he asked why she worked so much. And she did it all without ever letting on how tired she truly was.

But even then, Gregory knew. He could see it in the way she pinched her temples when she thought he wasn't looking or how her eyes glossed over at the kitchen table after dinner. She was saving for something, but she never said what it was. It wasn't a car—Gregory was sure of that because both of them took the bus back and forth without ever complaining. They didn't have enough money for a car, and honestly, a vehicle seemed like a luxury neither of them wanted. Whatever she was saving for, it was something more important, more personal. Gregory trusted her, though. She had always been the responsible parent, the one who stayed.

His mother's sacrifices were part of the reason Gregory didn't rebel or complain, even when things were at their tightest. He had friends who spent their weekends partying, who didn't have to worry about rent or the cost of groceries. But Gregory couldn't afford to slack off. He had to work. His mother's determination was like a guiding light for him, even when it felt like his world was falling apart. He was proud of her, even if she never said it herself. She had worked her way up from a CNA to a registered nurse after all those years, and it made him want to push harder, to succeed in ways that she hadn't been able to.

There were moments when Gregory felt the weight of it all—of being the "man of the house" when he was barely out of boyhood. He remembered coming home one night after a long shift at the mechanic shop. His hands were dirty, his arms sore, and his legs felt like lead. His mother was asleep on the couch, her work uniform still on, her shoes kicked off in the middle of the living room. He stood there, staring at her, feeling a surge of anger he couldn't explain. Not at her, but at the situation, at life.

Why did it have to be this hard? He would never say but sometimes he would feel it. Why couldn't they have a moment of peace? He almost gave up once. He almost walked into his boss's office at the shop and quit, just so he could stop feeling like the weight of the world was on his shoulders. But he didn't. Because every time he thought about quitting, he thought about his mother. He thought about how she never gave up on him, even when times were tough, even when his father had left. She had stayed, and that was enough to keep him going. She was his rock, and he owed her everything.

Gregory had dreams of his own, of course, but they were tucked away in the back of his mind, hidden behind the more immediate needs of survival. He wanted to get out of Brockton, to make something of himself. Maybe go to college, start a business, something where he wouldn't have to scrape by the way they had for so many years. But those dreams seemed distant, like something he wasn't sure he had the right to chase. Not yet, anyway. His mother came first.

Years later, Gregory would look back on those days and realize that they shaped him more than anything else. His father's absence had taught him how to be strong on his own. His mother's resilience had shown him the value of hard work and sacrifice. And even though they had struggled, even though life had been tough, Gregory knew that those years had built a foundation for the man he would become.

As he stood in the small park in Harlem, waiting for Tianna, he couldn't help but think about his own mother. About how much of her strength he had carried into his own life. He knew that his relationship with Tianna was special, and he didn't want to make the same mistakes his father had. He didn't want to leave anyone behind.

Lillian often found herself sitting in Richie's old room, the space frozen in time, like a museum of memories she couldn't let go of. The room was filled with remnants of his short life—hand-drawn pictures on the walls, toys scattered across the shelves, and the faint scent of his favorite bubblegum lingering in the air. Old model trains and planes Ralph built with the hopes that Richie would gravitate to that hobby as well. Each time she stepped inside, she was overwhelmed by a mix of nostalgia and grief. It was like being trapped in a place where time had stood still, where her son was forever four years old, his laughter echoing in the walls of her heart.

Those memories, so vivid and real, were both a comfort and a curse, hers to be exact. She wanted to keep every detail intact, to preserve the essence of her son. Yet, at the same time, each reminder was like a blade twisting in her gut, a cruel taunt of everything she had lost. Richie's laughter used to fill the house, a beacon of joy in their family's troubled world. Now, that joy was gone, replaced by an aching silence that only deepened as the years passed.

Lillian had tried to move on, to pack away the pieces of her grief, but every time she reached for something to put in a box—a toy car, a framed photo of Richie's gap-toothed smile—her hands would tremble, and she would falter.

She feared that letting go of his belongings would mean letting go of him. So, instead, she turned her pain inward, wrapping herself in it like a familiar blanket, something she could never truly shake off. Despite her best efforts, the memories would not let her go. At least once a week, the nightmare of that night returned, relentless and unforgiving. She would see Richie standing on the curb, his tiny figure illuminated by the streetlights, his eyes wide with fear. She'd hear the sickening thud of the car, feel the ground tremble under her feet, and then her own scream—piercing, primal, tearing through the night. No matter how many times she relived it, the horror never dulled.

But Tianna deserved to know. She deserved the chance to understand why her mother was the way she was—why Lillian had always seemed so distant, so tightly wound. It wasn't just grief; it was the crushing weight of a secret that had festered for years. Lillian had let her daughter believe that their fractured family was her father's fault, that his failures were to blame for the rift between them. She had allowed Ralph to take the fall because it was easier than facing her own mistakes.

Lillian's fingers lightly traced the edges of Richie's old drawing, a crayon creation of stick figures and bright, smiling suns. The sight of it stirred something deep inside her, and tears welled up in her eyes, threatening to spill over. For years, she had held her grief at bay, pretending to be strong—for Tianna, and for her own sense of stability. But now, the facade was cracking, and she realized she couldn't keep up the act any longer. The weight of all her unresolved pain felt almost unbearable.

In a rare moment of vulnerability, Lillian picked up the phone and dialed a co-worker, Merida. She invited her out for tea, perhaps at Brockton Mall or Westgate Mall. She was craving some company and a break from the loneliness that had been closing in on her. When they met up, Lillian couldn't help but feel a twinge of jealousy toward Merida—her husband was always so attentive and kind. But by the end of the afternoon, Lillian learned the truth. Merida's husband, though diligent about paying all bills, was controlling and overbearing. Ralph, it turned out, was a cheater, a liar, and a poor provider—but still somehow seemed to have it better than Lillian. As she removed her fluffy scarf at home, the confusion and uncertainty flooded in. She was unsure.

Chapter SEVEN

Disappointment had become a constant in Lillian's life. Each doctor's visit brought new updates about Ralph's condition—his memory was deteriorating, and he was starting to forget important details. The slurred insults, now almost a weekly occurrence, were another symptom of his decline. Yet, instead of driving them apart, these struggles seemed to tie them together in an unsettling way. It wasn't love or passion that bound them anymore, but something more complicated—trauma bonding. The shared hardship, the emotional strain, and Ralph's growing dependence on her had created a connection neither of them could fully escape. None of that mattered now. Her husband needed her.

Years of heavy drinking had caught up to him, accelerating his body's decay like a runaway train. Ralph moved sluggishly, he was not his normal self, the roundness of his belly and constant red rimmed eyes. He laughed bitterly about it when he still had the clarity to speak, saying, "Better to drink to forget than remember how terrible life was."

But it was more than that—it was a gradual, willful suicide that was eating him alive from the inside out. First, they diagnosed hepatic encephalopathy, a cruel disease that blurred his thoughts and confused his memory. Then, as if in punishment for all the years of numbing himself with alcohol, the encephalopathy progressed into early-onset dementia. But there were signs for a long time that something was not right.

Lillian remembered the day of that diagnosis vividly, sitting in the sterile white office as the doctor explained what to expect. “He’ll lose more than his memory. He’ll lose control of bodily fluids one day. There will be moments of clarity, but... prepare for a steady decline.” She nodded, taking notes she’d later throw away. The words sounded distant, a foreign language she didn’t want to translate into reality. Tianna was in her final year at Mass U, and Lillian didn’t think it was the best time to tell her daughter. It wasn’t a lie—she knew the news would only distract Tianna from school, flooding her mind with worry about a father who barely remembered her name.

The only bright side, if it could be called that, was that Ralph’s girlfriends stopped calling. They used to stop by, the older and bolder ones would stop by asking if the handy man was in. Before the diagnosis, they had wandered in and out of his life like stray cats, leaving traces of .99 cent perfume on the sofa cushions and lip prints on his glass tumblers. Lillian used to seethe with quiet rage, cursing Ralph’s audacity, wondering why she stayed. Her mother would threaten to shoot him.

Lillian softened, almost feeling sorry for him until he would act up.With his dementia worsening, they vanished, unwilling to linger around a man who no longer held any charm or use for them. Nurse maid was always the responsibility of the wife. Now, it was just Lillian, managing his medications and carting him to endless appointments. Ralph repaid her efforts with cursing and crude nicknames, calling her "Bitchy nurse" or "Nurse Ratchet."

"I'ma die drinking," he'd say sometimes, a twisted smile on his dehydrated lips.

"Well, since you've decreed it, you just might get your wish," Lillian would reply. It was a game, a sick call-and-response that made her skin crawl.

Each day was a waiting game—waiting for the next tantrum, the next round of spotty memories where Ralph would ask, What day is it again? What are you doing here? Each time he forgot who she was, she felt a piece of herself die. That pride thing was a beast, she needed to be remembered by a constant cheat. She did not know why her emotions betrayed her, maybe she still cared. But at present she'd swallow her grief, force a smile, and say, "It's just me, Lillian, your wife. I'm here to help."

"No, you ain't. You are here to Nag"

She made herself think of Tianna and how she'd react if she knew. Tianna, with her bright future and beautiful smile, deserved better than the shadow of a father Ralph had become. So, Lillian bore the weight alone, moving through each day like a soldier following orders. When the yelling subsided and Ralph would slump in his wheelchair, staring blankly out the window, she began planning his funeral months or possibly years than she was supposed to, but she wanted to be prepared.

Lillian thought about her own life. First, she lost her son because of him, stayed married because of Tianna and now Ralph was dying himself and there was no one else to help him. He was committing slow suicide, that was what alcoholism was, death. They were a strange entangled pair, bonded by dysfunction. And now he was dying. It wasn't a matter of if, but when.

But the strangest thing happened—she soon would no longer carry the weight alone.

Weeks later under twinkling lights from ceiling chandeliers. At dinner surrounded by Lillian's daughter, a few co-worker and friends. Deceptively sweet cocktails flowed, Janiyah became inebriated, feeling a sense of camaraderie, good food, good company. She had no idea that she downed so many. However, as the night wore on, the cocktails began to take their toll, and Janiyah found herself swaying slightly in her seat, her words starting to slur.

"Just one more, Janiyah!" Gregory urged, pouring her another drink with a teasing smile. He poured apple juice in her cup, she did not need any more alcohol. Janiyah was already nearly sliding out of her chair. Lillian looked at her distastefully, in her mind, coffee was needed.

"You're not going to let us drink alone, are you?"

Lillian signaled the waiter to bring her a cup. Janiyah's eyes slid over to Mrs. McQueen. And her face became serious.

"You and Tianna are so strong. How you both are surviving after the death of your son. That rainy night when you left out to find your husband. Richard slipped out while Tianna was sleeping. I pray every night that the drunk driver is caught."

Silence fell over the table, and the laughter died instantly. Tianna's eyes widened in shock, and Lillian froze, her fork hovering in mid-air. "Janiyah!" Lillian exclaimed, her voice a mix of horror and disbelief. "What are you talking about?"

Tianna felt her heart race as anger bubbled to the surface. "What do you mean she wasn't home?" she snapped, her voice trembling with disbelief. "You can't be serious!" Janiyah's head rolled back against the chair, and she groaned, struggling to focus. "I—I thought you knew…" she slurred, blinking slowly.

"And did you seriously just say that?" Tianna asked Janiyah, disbelief pouring out of her. "Mom, you let me believe it was Dad's fault all this time! Why would you keep this from me?"

Lillian's face paled, her hands trembling slightly. "Tianna, I can explain—"

“Explain what?” Her friend was unaware the proverbial cat was letting out the bag while she flirted while the man seated next to her. Tianna interrupted, her voice thick with frustration. “Why didn't you keep him safe? Why did you let him go outside alone? You let me believe it was Dad's fault this whole time!”

Lillian took a step forward, desperate to reach her daughter. “I didn’t want you to carry that burden! I thought I was protecting you!”

“But I’m carrying it anyway!” Tianna yelled, her frustration spilling over. “I’ve been living with this weight of YOURS for years, and now I find out you were out chasing my dad while he was cheating on you? It was you who left Richie! You were supposed to be there for him!”

Janiyah, realizing the gravity of what she had unleashed, tried to intervene. “Tianna, please, you don’t understand—”

“Shut up, Janiyah”

“Uhhh. Boy,” Janiyah’s date said, looking around the crowded room.

Lillian’s heart raced as she felt the ground shift beneath her. “I’m sorry,” she whispered, her voice barely audible. “I thought I was doing what was best for you. I never wanted to hurt you, Tianna.”

“I’m sorry Ms. Lillian,” remorse Lillian thought, now Janiyah is remorseful after the carnage, had seen Ralph behave the same way when he was drunk.

“I know,” Lillian said, her voice trembling. “But this isn’t just about you. This is about my daughter—my family. And I don’t know how to fix this.”

“I only had four cocktail drinks,” she answered, holding up two fingers.

Her date reminded her by holding up four fingers.

“You only had four very strong cocktails.”

“Shhh….,” Janiyah loudly whispered. She was holding her finger to his lips. For Tianna it was like watching her father. Placing her friend in the cab was challenging. Lillian was aggressively sitting Janiyah upright, it was not Janiyah’s fault that her mother lied.

“Ma. I got it.”

Tianna finished placing Janiyah in an upright position. She was furious, the chilly air sobered a friend, a little. ‘I’m sorry’, Janiyah eked out. It was much too late Tianna thought. Who gets that drunk around strangers. Janiyah would surely regret it in the morning.

Chapter EIGHT

Tianna was probably embarrassed and pissed, Janiyah thought, not just with her, but with everyone—her mother, her father, and maybe herself.

Hours later at home Janiyah reached for her phone, desperately hoping to make things right. She dialed Tianna's number, but after several rings, all she got was the automated voice apologizing for the missed call. It was too soon. She placed her phone down, frustrated. Tianna wasn't ready to talk, and Janiyah didn't blame her.

By eleven Sunday morning sun peering in the window was like cold water. Janiyah let embarrassment wash over her. She needed to make things right. Sitting at her small kitchen table, she stared at her phone, her fingers trembling as she hovered over the contact list. Detective Garcia. She hadn't spoken to him since the original investigation into Richie McQueen's death, but she remembered the way he handled things with care and diligence, even when the case went cold. Taking a deep breath, she dialed his number, hoping she wasn't making another mistake.

"Detective Garcia speaking," came the familiar gruff voice on the other end of the line. Janiyah cleared her throat, her voice shaky. "Hi, Detective, it's Janiyah. Janiyah Thompson. I don't know if you remember me, but I… I was there after Richie's accident. Tianna McQueen's best friend. We were kids, but..."

There was a pause, the kind that stretched long enough to make her doubt herself. "Yeah, I remember," Garcia replied, his tone measured but kind. "What can I do for you?"

"Is there any headway with the Richard McQueen hit-and-run case, actually it is an old case."

"Are you a family member? The mother or the sister?"

"No, a friend of the family."

"Well unfortunately. I can't give out any information about the case."

"I understand. I just want to help. " Janiyah whispered, her voice tight with emotion. "And Tianna's life has not been completely easy because of it. If you could look again, it might give her family some peace."

There was another long pause, followed by the sound of Garcia flipping through what Janiyah imagined were dusty case files. "Alright," he said at last, though his voice carried the resignation of a man who'd seen too many dead ends. "I'll review the file. No promises, though."

"Thank you, Detective," Janiyah breathed, her chest loosening a little as she ended the call. It wasn't much, but it was a start. Maybe this small step would make up for the damage she'd caused.

Later that evening, Janiyah found herself sitting across from Tianna in her cozy apartment. However, the air between them was heavy with unspoken words. Janiyah fidgeted, swirling her wine glass as she worked up the nerve to speak.

"I called Detective Garcia," she finally admitted, breaking the silence.

Tianna looked up, her face unreadable. "Why, did you? Her face annoyed. Do you know something we don't or are you making amends for messing up the dinner?"

Janiyah hesitated. "Because I messed up, Tee. I spilled secrets that weren't mine to tell, and I can't fix that. But I thought… Maybe if there was something new to uncover about Richie's accident, it might help. I just want to make things right."

Tianna sighed, her expression softening just a fraction. "It's not about fixing things, Janiyah. What's done is done. My brother's gone, for a long time now, and nothing's going to change that."

"I know," Janiyah whispered. "But I couldn't just sit by and do nothing."

For a moment, the only sound was the quiet clink of glass against wood as Tianna set her wine down. She met Janiyah's gaze, her eyes reflecting the years of hurt and frustration she'd carried. "We've all been stuck in the past, haven't we?"

Janiyah nodded, tears stinging her eyes. "Maybe it's time we all try to move forward."

The night ended with Janiyah still sulking, her cheeks flushed a soft pink after Tianna recounted the details of her date. And how he made excuses to leave early and how Gregory had stepped in, paying for her Uber and taking pictures of the driver's plate to ensure her safety. Janiyah seemed to appreciate the kindness of Gregory's effort, her silence hanging in the air as she stewed in her thoughts.

Tianna had learned early on not to depend on the love her parents offered, as it was often tainted by ridiculous rivalry. But despite all of this, she couldn't help but wonder if their brokenness had somehow shaped her own views on relationships and trust. It was hard to unlearn the damage they'd done, even if she tried to move forward in her own life.

She nearly wore a hole by pacing the living room, the photo frame clutched tightly in her hands. She had stumbled across it while searching for an old cookbook Tianna loved, tucked away in a drawer she rarely opened. The sight of the photo had stopped her in her tracks. She hadn't meant to linger, but now she couldn't let it go.

The sunlight slanted through the window, casting warm streaks across the room. It was morning again. The brightness felt at odds with the weight pressing on her chest. She traced her thumb over Tianna's smiling face in the photo, then over her own frozen smile—so practiced, so strained. Ralph stood beside them, his eyes distant even back then. And the glaring absence of Richard McQueen was like a knife in her side.

Her pacing slowed as she came to stand near the bay window. The bustling sounds of the neighborhood filtered in—children laughing, a dog barking, a lawnmower humming in the distance. It all seemed so ordinary, so unfair. How could life outside carry on when hers was frozen in that moment, the one where Richard McQueen was gone forever?

Lillian exhaled sharply and pressed the photo to her chest. "I should've been there," she murmured, her voice breaking. She turned toward the wall where a larger, framed family portrait hung. It was from the same day as the smaller photo, taken just minutes apart, yet it felt like a world away. In this one, Richard wasn't absent. He was running across the background, his little face blurred with joy because he couldn't sit still long enough for the shot. She had kept it on the wall all these years, convincing herself it wasn't a constant reminder of what she had lost.

But it was. It always has been. Her fingers trembled as she traced the outline of his face in the smaller photo. She felt the familiar weight of guilt press down on her chest like a stone. The memories she had tried to suppress for years came flooding back, unrelenting and vivid.

It was a cold, rainy night. Midnight, perhaps just past. Lillian had been restless, the pit in her stomach growing heavier as the hours dragged on. She had gone to bed earlier, expecting her husband, Ralph to join her at some point, but the bed beside her had stayed cold and empty. She'd assumed he'd fallen asleep on the couch, like he often did after coming home late from his so-called "meetings." But when she woke up to the sound of rain tapping against the window, she realized he wasn't there. He wasn't in the house at all.

She sat up, her heart pounding. This wasn't the first time Ralph had disappeared in the middle of the night. And deep down, Lillian knew where he was—or at least, where he wasn't. He wasn't at work, and he wasn't out running errands. He was with her. That other woman.

The rage burned in her chest, heating her from the inside even as the cold air seeped through the cracks in the house. She hadn't planned to leave, hadn't thought it through. She just needed to find him, to see for herself what she already knew. She had slipped on her nightgown and slippers and walked out into the rain, her resolve fueling her every step.

She didn't hear the soft creak of the back door as it closed behind her. She didn't hear the quiet shuffle of tiny feet padding across the wet grass.

Richie woke up shortly after she left. He had always been a light sleeper, and the sound of the rain mixed with the distant rumble of thunder stirred him awake. He rubbed his eyes and called out, "Mommy?" The house was silent. Too silent. He climbed out of bed, his favorite blanket trailing behind him, and walked down the hall. When he reached her room and saw her bed empty, panic set in.

"Mommy?" he called again, louder this time. Still no answer.

Richie went to the back door and saw it ajar, rain blowing in across the threshold. His little heart pounded. He stepped outside, clutching his blanket tightly. The rain soaked his small frame almost immediately, but he didn't care. All he cared about was finding her.

"Mommy? Where are you?" he cried, his voice trembling. He shuffled forward, the cold biting at his bare feet. And then he saw her—a blurry figure up the street, walking fast in the rain. Relief surged through him, and he ran as fast as his legs could carry him.

"Mommy! Wait for me!" he shouted, but his voice was too small to carry over the storm. Lillian didn't hear him. She was too focused, too consumed by her own anger and heartbreak.

Richie ran faster, his little legs straining to keep up. But the ground was slippery, and the rain blurred his vision. He didn't see the car until it was too late. The headlights were blinding, a sudden flash of light that swallowed him whole. The driver didn't see him either, not until the thud of impact jolted him to a stop. The car revved and was gone.

It wasn't until after she saw her friend gyrating on top of her husband with the nights off in the beauty salon window and slowly walked home. Blaring siren greeted her as she crossed a neighbor's backyard. Lillian returned only to realize something was wrong at her own house. The scream tore through the night, piercing and primal. It was her own voice.

She rounded the corner of the house just in time to see her son lying motionless in the street, his tiny body illuminated by the car's headlights. She ran toward him, her own legs threatening to give out beneath her. "No! Richie! No!"

The neighbors spilled out of their homes, drawn by the commotion. Someone banged on Tianna's door, rousing her from sleep. She stumbled outside, confusion and dread coursing through her veins. And there she saw it—her brother lying in the street, her mother collapsing beside him, wailing uncontrollably. A neighbor convinced her to wait for the paramedics. Lillians was afraid to move him, somewhere she heard that it could cause internal bleeding. Helpless, she watched Richie bleed out of his mouth feeling torn between gathering him in her arms and shaking him to consciousness, and sitting and waiting.

Lillian couldn't stop screaming. Not when the ambulance arrived, not when the police started asking questions, not even when they placed Richie's small, lifeless body on the stretcher. The sound tore through Tianna, ripping apart something inside her that could never be mended.

And then came the question. The detective, a middle-aged man with kind but weary eyes, looked directly at Lillian. "Can you tell us what happened, ma'am?"

Lillian froze. The words caught in her throat. She looked down at Richie, then back at the detective. Her lips parted, but the truth was too heavy to speak. How could she admit that she had left her children alone to chase after a man who didn't even love her? How could she own up to the fact that her own selfishness had cost her son his life?

"I... I don't know," she whispered finally, her voice barely audible. "I was taking out the trash." It was a lie, a damning unspoken confession. A lie said so many times that she deluded herself. And she had carried it with her ever since.

Now, standing in front of the family portrait, the weight of that night threatened to crush her. She had spent years burying the truth, hiding it from everyone—including herself. But she couldn't hide anymore. Not from Tianna. Not from herself.

"I left him," she whispered, her voice shaking. "I left him that night, and he followed me. If I had stayed...if I had just stayed… and now Tianna Knows everything."

Her knees buckled, and she sank to the floor, clutching the photo tightly to her chest. The sobs came fast and uncontrollably, each one pulling her deeper into the storm of her own guilt and regret. For the first time, she allowed herself to feel it all—to face the full weight of what she had done. Later after calming down, she was quiet and thought how Ralph must hate her as much as he hated himself.

And for the first time, she wondered if forgiveness was even possible.

The silence in the house felt suffocating, as if even the walls were holding their breath. Setting the smaller frame on the mantel, Lillian crossed the room and opened the back door, stepping onto the porch. The cool breeze hit her skin, and for a moment, she just stood there, letting it ground her.

"Richard McQueen," she said aloud, testing the weight of his full name. It felt strange and reverent on her tongue, as if invoking him might make him appear. "I am sorry I did not take care of you. I should have been home."

Her grip tightened on the doorframe as the tears came. They were different this time—less about grief and more about guilt. Richie had been the heart of their family, and now his absence felt like a void that could never be filled. But it wasn't just grief she carried; it was the secret she had kept from Tianna. She had spent years blaming Ralph for the unraveling of their family while burying her own culpability deep enough to almost believe it wasn't there.

"You let me believe it was Dad's fault this whole time!" Those were the last words her daughter said to her that night. How could she ever make things right again?

Chapter NINE

Tianna slumped onto the couch, staring blankly at the ceiling. How did they even get here? How did everything get so broken?

The silence of the apartment pressed in on her. It had once been her sanctuary, the place she went to escape the noise of her family's dysfunction. But now it felt suffocating, like the walls were closing in, amplifying the echoes of her thoughts.

Her phone buzzed on the coffee table, pulling her from her thoughts. She glanced at the screen. It was her mother.

Tianna hesitated, her thumb hovering over the screen. A part of her wanted to answer, to hear her mother's voice and maybe, just maybe, find some clarity. But another part of her—the stronger part—couldn't bear it. She wasn't ready to face Lillian, wasn't ready to forgive, or even to understand.

She let the call go to voicemail again, exhaling deeply as the screen went dark again. She needed time. Time to sort through the mess of emotions tangled inside her. Time to figure out what to do next. She wanted to block for a while but decided against it. What if her father had an emergency?

Tianna stuck her head out of the window this time, letting the sound of rustling leaves and the distant hum of traffic wash over her. For a moment, she allowed herself to just breathe.

Tianna's phone buzzed again. This time, it was a text message. She didn't need to look to know it was from her mother. The vibrations seemed to mirror the turmoil inside her, constant and nagging. She sighed, tucking the phone away in her jacket pocket, determined not to be pulled back into that emotional quicksand. Not yet.

For now, all Tianna wanted was distance—from the lies, from the pain, from everything that had been weighing her down. She knew she would eventually have to face her mother, but tonight wasn't that night. Tonight, she just needed a moment to breathe, to step away from the turmoil and give herself a break from the emotional burden she carried. The night air felt refreshing against her skin, providing a fleeting sense of solace that she desperately craved.

Meanwhile, Gregory's days had fallen into a repetitive rhythm, defined by the steady hum of his routine interspersed with occasional flickers of discontent. This monotony began to nudge him toward the notion of dating again, though uncertainty lingered in his mind. He liked Tianna, but they were still in the early stages of getting to know each other. In the quiet of his thoughts, he pondered the idea of celibacy, yet never fully committed to it. His struggle left him wondering whether he was exploring his options or merely avoiding the dating scene altogether.

Both Tianna and Gregory navigated their separate dilemmas, an unspoken connection began to form between them. While Tianna sought refuge from her emotional turmoil, Gregory grappled with his hesitations about moving forward.

Yet whenever Gregory did venture into dating, his uncertainty about taking his time often became a stumbling block. He found that some women, initially intrigued, would grow impatient upon discovering his hesitation and boundaries. Their impatience only reaffirmed his desire to take a step back, making meaningful connections seem even more elusive. Until of course seeing Tianna again. It wasn't that he wasn't open to intimacy—he just wasn't ready to give in to the expectation's others placed on him. Tianna, on the other hand, had been understanding, giving him space to figure things out.

The group 'date' had started innocently enough. What was meant to be a fun, casual evening of drinks and laughter had quickly spiraled into something far more uncomfortable. Tianna, her mother Lillian, Janiyah, Gregory, Mike and a couple of their mutual friends had gathered at a trendy dinner spot downtown. The atmosphere was lively, the music upbeat, and the conversation flowing freely—at least at first.

Well, he did attempt to persuade Janiyah to drink more water and juice instead of alcohol, but she dampened what could have been a pleasant evening. It was a bummer. She certainly had no business drinking that much or mentioning the night her friend's brother died. The night crashed and burned much like his love life.

Nevertheless, as he took applications for the job, he did not find any real applicants. They consistently revealed a shared theme—an inability to comprehend or respect his uncertainty. He found himself caught between two worlds, not fully committed to one lifestyle nor actively pursuing a relationship. The aggressive pushback he often encountered only deepened his reluctance, making the situation feel exhausting. He began to wonder if there was anyone out there who could appreciate his unique pace and his need for introspection.

Despite the complexity of his circumstances, Gregory found a peculiar sense of solace in the clarity gained from this period of self-reflection. Freed from these preoccupations, he discovered new depths of meaning in tasks that once seemed trivial, and a renewed energy began to surge within him. Projects that had languished on the back burner for months suddenly demanded his attention as he channeled his enthusiasm into home renovations.

The basement of his house, which he transformed into a vibrant studio and office space, was a testament to his dedication to personal growth. He enjoyed every moment of the process, from painting the walls to organizing his workspace. The remodeling of his mother's laundry room brought him a deep sense of satisfaction, as did the installation of security cameras for his tenants—acts that reflected his growing attention to detail and desire to improve the lives of those around him.

And yet, Gregory couldn't help but wonder, was this really where all his unused energy was going? He smirked to himself at the thought. Maybe this period of self-imposed distance was temporary, but for now, it seemed to work. He was channeling his energy into the things that mattered to him, at least for the time being.

When his backyard demanded attention, Gregory found himself back at the lumberyard, sifting through materials for the next phase of his renovation. Leaky faucet Gregory was on the case. Each visit to the lumberyard was an opportunity to immerse himself in the details of his latest project, and he reveled in the physicality of the work. The scent of fresh cut wood and the hum of the machinery became a comforting backdrop to his days, contrasting sharply with the sterile environment of his office.

Yet, amidst the monotony and the fulfillment of his various projects, there was one bright spot that consistently lifted his spirits: his conversations with Tianna. They exchanged numbers again, since that night. Their interactions had become a cherished part of his day. Tianna, now a rising star in her field, was not only a reminder of the past but also a beacon of positivity in Gregory's present. Their conversations ranged from light-hearted catch-ups to deeper discussions about life's intricacies, and Gregory looked forward to these moments with genuine anticipation.

Tianna's perspective, her wit, and her warmth provided a welcome escape from the repetitiveness of his daily life. Talking to her was more than just a pleasant distraction; it was a highlight that gave his day meaning and purpose. Her presence, even in the form of these conversations, reminded him of the connections that mattered most. It was during these exchanges that Gregory felt a sense of genuine connection and understanding, something he had been missing in his interactions with others. As Gregory continued to navigate his self-imposed celibacy and the challenges it brought, he found himself increasingly introspective.

Across town, Tianna sat in her apartment, her mind drifting back to that same night over and over again. She was exhausted—tired of feeling stuck, tired of the memories that wrapped around her like chains. She wanted to let go, to move on, but how could she when there were still so many questions left unanswered? Every time she thought of Richie, it wasn't just the pain of losing her brother—it was the frustration of knowing that the person responsible was still out there, living their life, unpunished.

The feeling of being trapped was like a heavy fog that she couldn't shake. It settled over her every morning when she woke up and lingered in the quiet moments before sleep. Even her successes felt somehow hollow. She felt guilty, survivor's remorse. And her achievements are muted by the echoes of a past that refused to let her go. Tianna thought of her mother, Lillian, who had never fully recovered, whose grief was like a shadow that stretched across their lives.

When she closed her eyes, Tianna saw Lillian's face on the day Richie died—a mask of horror and disbelief, her hands trembling as she reached out to a son she couldn't save. And now, decades later, that same look was there every time Tianna saw her mother. Lillian hadn't aged so much as she had withered under the weight of her sorrow. Her grief had turned into a kind of stubborn refusal to accept the world as it was, because to move on would mean letting go of Richie—and how could she ever do that when the person who took him from her was still free?

Tianna was absorbed with work, burying herself in her clients' needs, and giving little thought to the dinner party that had gone so wrong. The chaos from that night seemed distant, fading into the background as she threw herself into her professional life. Calls from her mother and Janiyah went unanswered, each ring reminding her of the tangled mess she didn't want to untangle just yet. She needed a break, a vacation—a place where she didn't have to think about anything or anybody. A beach, perhaps, with the sound of waves drowning out all the noise. Or maybe, she thought, someone could come with her. Maybe Gregory.

Just the two of them, away from everything, where she could finally catch her breath and sort through the whirlwind of emotions that had taken hold of her. It seemed like a distant dream, but in the quiet of her office, it was the only thing that offered any comfort.

The frustration of not knowing gnawed at her, a constant reminder of everything that was lost. She didn't just want closure; she needed it. She needed to know who was responsible, to make sense of the senseless, to find some way to put the pieces of her family back together, even if they'd never fit quite the same.

Janiyah finally reached Tianna at her apartment. Was this the second apology? She did not know, but Janiyah telling was part of the issue, but her mother finally admitting to lying overshadowed everything. Tianna invited her over, she poured them both wine. The warmth of the room felt stifling as Janiyah sat across from Tianna, her eyes downcast. The alcohol had long worn off, leaving behind a haze of regret. She fidgeted with her glass, knowing the gravity of what she had shared the night before. "Tianna, I'm so sorry," she began, her voice barely above a whisper. "I didn't mean to spill everything like that."

"No. Tee. this is all my fault."

"Even though my mother lied, at some point I have to forgive her. She made a mistake that she had to live with. Both of my parents were at fault. You just told what you knew. She is still hurting. And I can't punish a woman still mourning a dead son, even if she is at fault. I just need to process this and that takes time."

"I am so sorry Tianna."

"I know Janiyah, but that still does not bring my brother back to me or my parents."

Tianna tears slid off her face and into her wine. The night ended with tears and outbursts. But still did not give Tianna any idea how to move forward with her parents.

Chapter TEN

Tianna decided to go out with Gregory, hoping to distract herself from her mother's lies and Janiyah's big mouth. The first dinner with their friends had been a disaster—Janiyah's careless gossip and the awkward tension had left Tianna feeling exposed and humiliated.

In the quiet moments after, when life was not so hectic their phone conversations had become a lifeline. It was nice to have someone to talk to and confide in, and Gregory had become that person. His patience and understanding had given her the confidence to consider another date with him. Feeling numb from the emotional turmoil, a one-on-one evening with him seemed like exactly what she needed. When he picked her up, he surprised her with flowers, and she couldn't help but smile, grateful for his thoughtfulness. The simple gesture felt like a small but meaningful reassurance that maybe things could be different this time.

Dinner at Footprints in Harlem was the perfect setting for them to reconnect, and this time it was just the two. The cozy ambiance, with its warm lighting and eclectic decor, offered an intimacy that made them both feel at ease. Initially, they had planned a larger group outing, but circumstances had shifted, leaving just the two of them. While Gregory had hoped for a light-hearted evening, he couldn't shake the memory of their previous "group date," which had gone awry. That night, he had ventured into personal territory too soon, leaving them both feeling vulnerable and exposed.

As they settled into their meals, a slight tension lingered in the air. Tianna, her eyes sparkling with curiosity, asked about his recent adventures. Gregory felt the familiar urge to share more than surface-level pleasantries, but he was cautious. The conversation took a serious turn almost immediately, dampening the mood. He found himself revealing feelings he had buried—his fears about commitment, struggles with self-doubt, and hopes for a future that seemed increasingly uncertain.

Tianna listened intently, her expression shifting from light-hearted amusement to genuine concern. As she began to share her own stories of navigating love and relationships, Gregory realized how much they both carried. The air was thick with unspoken words and emotions, and he worried that they had rushed into heavy topics too quickly.

"Yeah, like what?" Tianna replied, a hint of a smile tugging at her lips, encouraging him to take the lead.

"So… what is your idea of a comfortable lie?"

"Seriously?" she laughed. "There are no comfortable lies," Tianna clarified, though she struggled to find the right words to shift the mood.

"Lies are manipulative," she continued, her voice edged with tension.

"Even little white lies?" he asked.

"Yes, especially those. Remember the dinner fiasco. They destroy lives." Tianna's response suggested a personal connection to the topic, perhaps related to her thesis on trauma bonds.

"Yeah, your friend Janiyah, right?"

"Yes," Tianna hesitantly responded. "Thank you for trying to take her drinks away. Her date did not care one way or the other."

Then they were both quiet. She felt tense. What the hell she thought, I just left work seeing patients. A first "date" wasn't the time for such profound discussions. This dinner was different. This bothered her. She missed the straightforward questions like: Are you married? Were you ever married? Will you ever get married? Do you have children? Do you want children? Have you had issues with drinking, drugs, arrests, or bankruptcy? And the other big question, are you hetero?

Seeing him again was strange after that night. But in a crowd, she would have recognized his height, smile, and voice anywhere. He was handsome. But this analytical date is not what she had in mind, since they were midway through it, she decided to hold off judgement. It made sense why Janiyah had been so secretive about him coming to dinner; she knew it would be a pleasant surprise and possibly lead to an opportunity for Tianna, who had been working as an administrative assistant at their midtown office. Janiyah and Michael were dating, which helped break the ice and allow Gregory and Tianna to reconnect. He worked at the radio station, doing voice overs for commercials and reading audiobooks. It was a pleasant surprise until the impromptu drama.

Since his father ran like a coward those insecurities could have stayed with him, making him bitter. And for a while Gregory blamed himself for not being good enough. He assumed his mother blamed herself too, carrying the weight of rejection, however those feelings did not last. It made them stronger. And shaped Gregory's personality. He tries to see things from a woman's point of view, mostly because of what his father put them through.

"Maybe we should lighten things up," Gregory suggested, attempting to inject some levity into the conversation. "What's the most ridiculous thing you've ever done on a date?"

Tianna laughed, the tension in her shoulders easing a bit. "Oh, there's a long list. But I'll start with the time I accidentally spilled red wine all over my date's white shirt. He didn't take it well!"

Gregory chuckled, picturing the scene, and felt the mood shift back toward the playful banter they had both enjoyed in the past. They exchanged funny anecdotes, their laughter gradually filling the space between them.

A wave of relief washed over him. She still remembered him. As they settled into their seats, he couldn't help but wonder about her mother. How was she doing? Did she ever forgive him for his past mistakes? He hesitated to ask, fearing that it might bring up painful memories.

But as the evening continued, they found a balance between vulnerability and light-heartedness. Tianna realized that amidst the chaos in her life, sharing laughter and experiences with Gregory felt like a breath of fresh air. Their connection deepened, and she understood that while they both had burdens to carry, they could also lean on each other for support. She found that he did not need to sit on her couch. He is just human. And she might consider a second one. Maybe.

At first when Gregory went on his date with Tianna, he wondered if she would still recognize him after all these years. She was pleased, he saw it in her eyes. He wondered how her mother was doing although for some reason he did not ask. Her father was another story. He did not respect or tolerate men who beat up their spouses. Gregory knew it was all about control. But instead of ending the evening in her bed, Gregory left with a soft kiss on her cheek at her doorstep. And even though she was interested, Tianna wanted to avoid any lingering resentment from his past relationships; she didn't need the drama.

ELEVEN

Dishes needed to be done, again. Lillian shrugged her shoulders to no one in particular as she washed the dishes. It's not like Ralph was going to do them. His mood swings were unpredictable, she knew this. He ran hot then cold like faucet water. And after a bad day, he'd take out his frustrations on Lillian, leaving her constantly on edge. She learned to adapt to his behavior, hoping that things would improve, especially after their son Richie's death. But even as she tried to be patient with him, the weight of their shared grief only seemed to deepen the chasm between them.

Ralph married Lillian Davis right after high school. Determined not to let her slip away to someone else—especially a college boy—he convinced her to stay in Brockton and attend community college. Lillian had dreams of going further with her education, but Ralph's relentless persuasion kept her grounded. She became pregnant with their first child, Tianna, during her first year of community college, and soon after, they were married in his mother's backyard, despite Lillian's own mother's objections.

Her mother's tears that day were not those of joy but of sorrow and disappointment. She knew that Lillian was giving up a brighter future for the promise of love that Ralph couldn't possibly fulfill. Yet, Lillian felt she had no choice—Ralph's charm and promises of stability were too convincing, and by then, she was already pregnant. But in an accident at work before he was deemed a permanent employee. And deemed his fault, there would be no workman's compensation, just years of disability checks.

Years later, the dream of a happy family life had long faded. Ralph's demeanor changed more drastically after Richie's tragic untimely death. Her husband's volatility became more pronounced. He swung from one extreme to another—warm affectionate one moment, then cold and distant the next. The grief seemed to magnify his insecurities and resentments, which he took out on Lillian.

"Lillian stole all my good years," he would joke bitterly to his friends, masking the pain of a life that hadn't gone the way he'd planned. Despite his outward charm and good looks, he felt his youth slipping away, suffocated by the responsibilities he had tried so hard to avoid. Maybe that is why she started cheating. Looking in the mirror, she saw imperfections, which added to the excuses she gave him.

Lillian, meanwhile, was overwhelmed with guilt and grief over Richie's death. She often wondered if staying with Ralph was a mistake, but she convinced herself that it was for the sake of their daughter, Tianna. She didn't want to tear their family apart, even if it meant sacrificing her own happiness.

Tianna, who was still young at the time, seemed to idolize her father despite his flaws. Lillian watched helplessly as her daughter sided more with Ralph, seeing him as a hero while Lillian was cast as the nagging mother. It was a bitter pill to swallow, knowing that the man who had caused so much pain was still somehow the one Tianna looked up to.

As the years passed, Ralph's behavior continued to deteriorate. His health declined rapidly due to his heavy drinking, and he was eventually diagnosed with hepatic encephalopathy, a condition that affected his memory and cognitive abilities. Even as his physical state weakened, his bitterness toward Lillian only seemed to grow.

One day, as Lillian drove Ralph to a doctor’s appointment, she glanced over at him slumped in the passenger seat, barely sober. She couldn’t help but think about the life they could have had if things had been different. If Ralph had been a different man or if she had made different choices.

“Why do you stay with him?” people would ask her from time to time, and Lillian never had a simple answer. She stayed for Tianna. She stayed because she couldn’t bear the thought of breaking apart what little remained of their family. And, perhaps, she stayed because somewhere deep down, she still hoped for the man she once believed Ralph could be.

Lillian’s relationship with her daughter remained strained. Tianna, now older and more aware of her parents' flaws, began to see through the facade. The more Tianna grew, the more she questioned

Lillian's choices—why she stayed with Ralph, why she put up with his

"Yes, I stayed because of you," Lillian admitted one evening, her voice trembling. It seemed Lillian was making excuses way before Tianna found out she lied about being home, if Lillian was being honest with herself.

"But I also stayed because I thought I could fix him. I thought I could make him see what he was doing to us, to this family. And I thought if I could just hold on long enough, things would get better. But I was wrong, Tianna. I was so wrong.It does not change what happened but, it's the truth."

"But mommy, you shouldn't have. You were not happy."

Tianna's face softened, seeing the vulnerability in her mother's eyes for the first time. She realized that her mother wasn't just the strict figure she had always known; she was a woman who had made sacrifices and lived with regrets that she could never fully express.

"You and Richie were the best thing that Ralph and I had." At that moment Tianna did not know what to say. Everything else seemed meaningless to say. Her mother was also still in mourning after all this time. Tianna did not feel right to continue to punish her. Lillian knew she was wrong and would do that that night back if she could. But none of them could.

Ralph's condition continued to worsen, and the reality of their situation became clear to Lillian. Tianna was grown; she was no longer staying for Tianna's sake but out of a sense of duty to a man who had taken so much from her. His arrogance, his neglect, and the years of emotional distance weighed heavily on her heart, but now he was helpless—reduced to a fragile, fading figure of the man she once resented. She would care for him in his final days, not because of love but because of a promise she made to herself to never abandon her family, no matter how broken they were.

Each time she tended to his needs, wiping his brow or adjusting his IV, she reminded herself that this was her penance. In the quiet moments when Ralph would fall asleep, she often wondered whether forgiveness was even possible, or if she was merely going through the motions to keep from feeling the sting of guilt.

There was the handkerchief his half-brother liked to borrow from him and of course, she kept the flower arrangements minimal. He was allergic, after all. How he would smell them in a casket, who knew? But some details, even in death, were non-negotiable.

How could Lillian have known it would take a year and a half from the day she picked out the coffin? By then, Ralph had forgotten how to walk, his brain sending out signals his body no longer obeyed. Sometimes he'd sit in that damned wheelchair by the window, staring at a world he no longer remembered, no longer belonged to. Sometimes, he'd mumble something, a fractured piece of the man he used to be breaking through the fog. She would listen, heart heavy with the knowledge that there would be a day when he wouldn't say anything.

All the preparations were in place, down to the obituary pamphlets she left unprinted, waiting for the exact date to be filled in. It was a quiet sort of acceptance, an exhaustion that dulled the edges of her grief. When the end finally came, less than two years after the dementia diagnosis, it felt more like an overdue relief than a loss.

Chapter TWELVE

The progress was fragile, but it was progress nonetheless. Lillian wasn't perfect, and Tianna knew there would be setbacks—more moments of silence, more difficult conversations ahead. But this—a real conversation, not hidden behind walls or masks—was something new. Something worth fighting for. Tianna had spent so many years bracing for the worst from her mother, but now, maybe, just maybe, she could finally begin to believe in the possibility of healing.

While her mind often circled around her family's issues, Tianna's professional life demanded her full attention. Her work, once a source of fulfillment, had slowly become a way for her to escape, to bury herself in something that required no emotional investment. The days blurred into one another, filled with endless stacks of summaries, briefs, and referrals. She was good at what she did—her clients often praised her for her attention to detail and her unflinching commitment to their needs. But there was a hollowness to it all. She had fallen into a routine, a cycle of work that provided comfort only through its predictability. Each evening, after long hours spent at her desk, she would retreat to her apartment, where a glass of wine became her ritual, a small solace before the grind began again.

Lately, though, things have been quieter. The chaos of her earlier years—her broken family, her own emotional turmoil—had quieted down, and Tianna found herself craving peace. Her apartment, once a place of constant tension, had become a sanctuary. She enjoyed the stillness, the solitude. It was a far cry from the chaos of her past, but it was exactly what she needed. Peace had become her new goal. She didn't need excitement or adventure; she just needed to catch her breath.

But as she sat at her desk one evening, sipping from her glass of wine and staring blankly at her computer screen, her thoughts began to drift. She had been working with wealthy clients for years, providing them with legal counsel, guiding them through complex financial and personal issues. It was a good job, and it had allowed her to live comfortably, even luxuriously. But now, something had begun to shift inside her. She realized, with a jolt, that her community—her very own community—was underserved.

Her mind flashed back to a conversation she'd had with one of her neighbors a few weeks earlier. Ms. Roberson, who lived two floors below, had stopped her in the hallway. "I was wondering if you knew of any places I could send my grandson," she had said. "He's got so much anger these days. Ever since his daddy left...he doesn't talk to nobody. He just holds it all in." Tianna had been caught off guard by the question. "I'm not sure," she replied honestly. "Maybe a local community center?" Ms. Roberson had sighed.

"Tried that. It's just not enough. They mean well, but the kids don't feel like anybody's really listening to them, you know? They need more than a basketball court and a couple of snacks. They need somebody who understands what they're going through."

That conversation had lingered in Tianna's mind ever since. Ms. Roberson's grandson wasn't the only one. There were so many others like him—young boys and girls growing up in an environment that didn't see them, didn't hear them, didn't believe in them. The community centers were doing their best, but they weren't equipped to deal with the deeper emotional wounds these kids carried. And the schools? Overcrowded, underfunded, and too quick to label kids as "troublemakers" rather than understanding their pain.

Tianna knew she couldn't fix everything. She couldn't solve the problems of an entire city, and she couldn't change the world overnight. But she felt a growing sense of responsibility, a gnawing urgency to do something. She had the skills, the knowledge, and the resources to make a difference. The question was how. How could she balance her successful legal career with the desire to help those who truly needed it? It was a delicate balance, one that required her to confront the tension between her comfortable life and the reality of the people who lived just blocks away, struggling to survive.

The idea began to take shape slowly, almost imperceptibly at first. What if there was a space—one that wasn't just about keeping kids off the streets but about truly empowering them? A place where they could be heard, where their pain could be acknowledged and healed? What if there was a way to provide counseling sessions specifically tailored to the challenges these communities faced? Not just for the kids, but for their families too?

Tianna imagined a center—no, a movement—dedicated to this cause. Something like "Better Me" or "Better Health," but rooted deeply in the realities of undervalued communities. The name didn't matter yet. What mattered was the purpose: to give people like Ms. Roberson's grandson the tools to navigate their emotions, to dream beyond their circumstances, to believe in themselves. She pictured counselors trained not just in therapy but in cultural competency, people who understood the unique pressures of growing up in underserved neighborhoods. There would be workshops for parents, mentorship programs for teens, even sessions on financial literacy to help families break the cycle of poverty.

Maybe it wasn't a concrete plan yet, but it was something. For the first time in a long while, Tianna felt a spark of excitement—a sense of purpose that went beyond her own comfort. She didn't have all the answers, but she knew she had to try. Maybe it was time to stop viewing her work as just a means of survival, and start using her talents for something bigger than herself. The city needed advocates. It needed people who cared, who were willing to fight for the voiceless. Maybe it was time for Tianna to be one of those people.

Chapter THIRTEEN

Tianna glanced at herself in the mirror for the third time, adjusting her scarf as Janiyah waited impatiently by the door. "You look fine, Tee. Come on, we're going to miss all the good stuff!" Janiyah urged, already halfway out of Tianna's apartment.

Tianna smirked and followed her out. The weather in Manhattan was brisk, but the city buzzed with its usual energy, the streets alive with tourists and locals alike. Today, they were determined to lose themselves in the simple joy of shopping—a distraction Tianna desperately needed after the emotional rollercoaster she'd been on.

Janiyah had been a constant presence in her life, and after everything with her mother's revelation about Richie's death, Tianna appreciated the light-heartedness of a day spent with her best friend. No heavy talks, no deep emotions—just shopping, laughter, and the endless array of store windows that lined Fifth Avenue.

"I think I need a whole new wardrobe for the new job," Janiyah declared, linking arms with Tianna as they crossed the street. "Something that says 'I'm professional, but I still know how to have fun.'"

"Isn't that what you said last time?" Tianna teased, raising an eyebrow. "You've got more clothes than me, and I work in an office."

"Non- Profits are nothing to sneeze at and you can never have too many clothes," Janiyah said, grinning. "Besides, a shopping spree is exactly what we need to clear our minds."

Tianna chuckled, grateful for the distraction. As they ducked into a high-end boutique, the sound of soft jazz and the hum of chatter filled the air. The space was open and luxurious, racks of expensive clothing draped like works of art. Janiyah made a beeline for a row of colorful dresses, while Tianna lingered near a display of winter coats.

For a moment, Tianna's thoughts drifted back to the complexities of her relationship with her mother. She had decided not to confront Lillian yet. After all, time was what she needed to process everything, and this outing with Janiyah was a welcome escape.

"Hey, what about this one?" Janiyah called, holding up a bold red dress. "Too much?"

Tianna laughed, shaking her head. "Depends on where you're going. Trying to catch someone's attention?"

Janiyah wiggled her eyebrows. "Maybe. But first, I'm catching some discounts." She darted off toward the fitting rooms, leaving Tianna with a quiet moment to herself.

As Tianna browsed through the racks, she felt a sense of calm settling in. The simplicity of the day—the routine of shopping, trying on clothes, and indulging in small talk—was exactly what she needed. For a few hours, she could forget about family drama, about Richie, about everything weighing her down. They had just finished at the boutique and stepped back onto the busy sidewalk when Janiyah suddenly nudged Tianna. "Look over there."

Tianna followed Janiyah's gaze and spotted someone familiar across the street. It was Maxine—her old friend—walking quickly, her head slightly bowed, as if trying to avoid being noticed. But it wasn't just her hurried steps that caught Tianna's attention—it was the short, stout, but undeniably handsome man at Maxine's side. He was older, dressed sharply, and clearly trying to keep pace with Maxine's flustered movements.

"Wait. Hold up. Is that… Maxine?" Janiyah asked, her brow furrowed.

Tianna squinted. "No way! It *is* her. Look at her trying to hide."

Maxine glanced up at that very moment and spotted them both. She froze for a split second, her face going pale before she flashed an awkward smile, waving weakly. She was caught. The man beside her looked confused, glancing between Maxine and the two women across the street. He actually stood on tippy toes to get a better view.

Janiyah, never one to hold back, grinned widely and gave Maxine a thumbs up. Tianna followed suit, laughing as they both waved in exaggerated encouragement. Maxine, clearly embarrassed but unable to help herself, smiled back. Her face relaxed as she realized they weren't about to make the situation worse.

"Who is that guy?" Tianna whispered as Maxine and her companion disappeared into a small café.

Janiyah shrugged, still grinning. "No idea. But judging by her reaction, I'd say it's someone she didn't want us to see her with. But he was cute, just a little bit height challenged."

"There you go."

"What ?, I said he was cute."

"Maxine's always been a bit of a nuisance and a mystery," Tianna mused. "Maybe she'll finally tell us the whole story."

"Or maybe not," Janiyah said, chuckling. "She likes to keep us guessing, while talking about our dating choices."

They continued down the street, the encounter with Maxine providing them with plenty of material for jokes as they wandered from one store to the next. It was nice, Tianna realized, to have moments like this—moments where she wasn't burdened by everything happening in her life, where she could simply enjoy the day with Janiyah and laugh at the absurdity of life's little surprises.

After a few more stops and a quick bite to eat, the sun began to dip lower in the sky. The streets glowed with the warm light of storefronts and street lamps, and Tianna found herself feeling lighter than she had in weeks.

"Hey, thanks for this," Tianna said, as they made their way back toward the subway. "I really needed it."

Janiyah looped her arm through Tianna's, smiling. "That's what best friends are for. Anytime you need to get away, you know I'm down."

As they boarded the A train, Tianna's phone buzzed with a new text. It was from her mother, she had her own special tone. She asked if they could meet for coffee soon. Tianna stared at the message for a moment, her thumb hovering over the screen. She wasn't ready yet—but maybe, soon, she would be. Janiyah noticed the look on her face but didn't say anything. She simply gave Tianna's arm a squeeze, offering her quiet support.

Tianna sat on the plaid blanket, her back resting against the smooth bark of an oak tree, trying to push away the awkwardness lingering from their last date. The small park in Harlem was a pocket of serenity amid the bustling city, with its winding paths and lush greenery offering a perfect escape. Gregory unpacked the wicker basket beside her, his movements slow, as if testing the waters after their strained evening.

"I thought we could use a reset," he said, offering a tentative smile. After their first date she was not interested in seeing him again. And since her mother let the cat out the bag about Richie, Tianna was overwhelmed. Tianna returned it, grateful for the effort. "Yeah, last time… let's just say it wasn't our best moment."

Gregory chuckled, setting down two sandwiches wrapped in parchment paper. "I'm not usually the guy who talks about 'comfortable lies' on a first date."

Tianna laughed softly, the tension between them melting under the warm sunlight. "It was intense," she agreed, "but maybe we needed to have that conversation. I mean, honesty's a big deal." Gregory nodded.

"True. But I should've just asked what your favorite color was or if you prefer dogs or cats." He handed her a lemonade from the; cooler.

"I bought lemonade, by the way. I figured we could keep it simple this time." Tianna took the drink, her fingers brushing his. "Simple sounds good."

As they ate, the breeze rustled the leaves above them, carrying the soft laughter of children playing nearby. Tianna found herself relaxing, the unease from their previous date fading with every bite. Gregory, too, seemed more at ease, his shoulders losing the stiffness she'd noticed before.

"Can I ask you something?" he said after a while.

Tianna glanced up, meeting his gaze. "Sure."

"Why didn't you just walk out during the date? I mean, it was pretty bad," he said with a hint of self-deprecation.

Tianna thought for a moment, a smile tugging at her lips. "Because I knew that wasn't you. You were trying too hard to impress me with deep questions instead of just being yourself. I liked the guy who picked out this perfect picnic spot more than the one who asked me about 'comfortable lies.' Gregory laughed, relief washing over his face. "Well, I'm glad you didn't give up on me."

He raised his lemonade. "Here's to less awkward dates." Tianna clinked her glass against his. "And more picnics."

As the sun dipped lower, casting a golden hue over the park, the two of them settled into an easy rhythm, letting the simple joy of the moment speak for itself.

Chapter FOURTEEN

The next morning, Tianna woke up feeling unusually calm. The previous day's outing had done more than just distract her—it had reminded her of life outside the weight of her family's secrets. Janiyah's laughter still echoed in her ears, and she smiled at the memory of Maxine's flustered expression. She was literally the deer caught in headlights.

But today was different. Today, she couldn't ignore the message from her mother any longer. Lillian had reached out, and Tianna knew that, eventually, they would have to face everything that had been left unsaid. For now it was too much work and her hands were filled with patients. On occasion Tianna did feel lonely and overwhelmed.

Her mind wandered to Gregory. His interest in Tianna was evident not only from the questions he asked her but also in the way he occasionally gazed at her, seemingly lost in thought. Each time their conversations turned to laughter, he couldn't help but admire how her natural curls framed her face, dancing softly with the breeze. He noted how her eyes sparkled with joy, especially when she spoke passionately about her dreams and aspirations. There was something enchanting about the way her enthusiasm radiated, lighting up the space around her.

He found himself captivated by the effortless beauty she possessed. It wasn't just her appearance that drew him in; it was the authenticity she exuded, a genuine spirit that made everyone around her feel at ease. Her laughter, infectious and melodic, had a way of lifting his mood, and he often caught himself wishing he could make her smile more often.

Gregory felt an undeniable urge to spend more time with her, to delve deeper into the layers of her personality. Each encounter left him wanting more, igniting a desire to learn about her interests, fears, and dreams. He envisioned long walks where they could share stories and explore each other's worlds. The thought of being able to witness her genuine reactions to life filled him with excitement. Yet, despite his growing feelings, a sense of hesitation lingered in his mind. He worried about how to express his admiration without overwhelming her. Would she feel the same spark he felt, or would his feelings remain one-sided?

As he pondered these questions, he realized that he wanted to create moments that would make her laugh and help her see the beauty in the mundane. He longed for those fleeting moments that could turn into cherished memories, each one drawing them closer together. Gregory was determined to navigate this budding connection, eager to discover where it might lead.

One evening, he mustered the courage to suggest a day trip to Martha's Vineyard. Since they both were from Massachusetts and had never been, it seemed like a perfect idea. Tianna smirked, knowing a "day trip" to Martha's Vineyard would likely take more time than that. It would likely become a weekend trip. She had always wanted to visit but never had the chance. Her schedule was packed, but she considered clearing it for the trip.

Why wouldn't he? Gregory asked suddenly, second-guessing his suggestion. He knew Tianna needed a break; most of their conversations revolved around work and her strained relationship with her mother, not about friends or new experiences. He hoped this trip would give her something positive to focus on and maybe even brag about.

Gregory, who had dated a lot and sometimes played both the good and bad guy, felt emotionally lonely and hoped Tianna could help fill that void. Though he never thought it was too soon to date her, he was eager to try. Tianna, though uncertain, agreed to the idea with a smile. “Okay,” she said, “When are we going?”

He looked relieved and smiled. “I'll handle the planning.” He had a friend in the music industry with a summer house on the Vineyard, which he had access to ever since covering for him when he took his girlfriend to France. It was a bit sleazy, but Tim was relieved to escape the griping of his wife, Elizabeth. Minding his business he asked not to know about anything else. That weekend was just for Greg and Tee.

They decided on a town called Oak Bluffs, known for its rich Black culture and history—a perfect short vacation spot. Tianna, who had never been to Martha's Vineyard but always wanted to visit, was excited. Despite rarely drinking beer, she enjoyed three while sitting on the beach with Gregory. The house they stayed in was incredible, complete with a housekeeper. They initially planned to stay just one night but decided to extend their stay for the weekend. Tianna canceled her earlier hotel reservation, grateful for Gregory's efforts.

Gregory's kisses on her fingertips are tender and captivating. The warm kisses that travelled from her neck to her mouth were gentle and unhurried. His gentle kisses warmed Tianna from head to toe, rekindling feelings she hadn't experienced in ages. "Whoa," Tianna put a bit of space between them. And slow them both down. She had never been to Martha's Vineyard and she wanted to sightsee. She was curious about what other surprises Gregory had planned. The campfire date was a delightful addition to their local weekend trip. The summer home was spacious and serene, offering a refreshing break from the island's tourist spots.

When Gregory unpacked the items for s'mores, Tianna asked about them with a smile, looking more beautiful as she relaxed. They entered the estate through the kitchen, soaked from a warm rain. Despite the rain, the house was stunning with its floor-to-ceiling windows. The deck was wet, but they continued inside. They ended up on the tiled floor, kissing and undressing each other. Huger wild tongue foreplay replaced the tender kisses. Their passion escalated quickly. Sloppy warm wet mouths devoured each other. Tianna remembered ripping his shirt and him playful biting her inner thighs then finally gripping her hip bones leveraging himself before diving deep and sending them both into an abyss of pleasure.

Although their lovemaking was intense and urgent, it was tender and authentic. Besides it being a passionate experience he was thorough and thoughtful. Gregory was determined not to let Tianna's first experience with him be anything less than extraordinary. Afterwards he walked to retrieve their wet clothes from the floor. Held out his hand and helped her to her feet. They moved to the bathroom which featured a double shower and a bathtub for two. Love play ensued at a slow and steady pace under warm rain. When he turned her to face the wall Gregory bent down to suckle the soft flesh at the back of her neck. He then changed direction by sitting on the shower bench and pulled her on top of him. By the fourth wave she knew she had a problem and his name was Gregory Michael Stevens.

Tianna, still buzzed from the beer and while in the afterglow of their lovemaking, initially thought she just wanted to sleep. But Gregory was attentive, placing her leg on a bench and tenderly soaping her. His touch led to another round of lovemaking, this time more deliberate and savoring each moment. Tianna experienced a new level of ecstasy, tears rolling down her face. They finally rinsed off and went to bed.

As Gregory leaned in for a kiss, Tianna, exhausted, thought he wanted more. Instead, he kissed the top of her head and held her close.

Tianna nestled in, appreciating the comfort and peace. Gregory's low, rumbling voice asked if she was asleep. "Yes, Gregory," she replied.

"Do you know why I asked you all those questions about trust?" he asked.

"You don't have to explain, Gregory. It's okay. You completely redeemed yourself," Tianna responded. He wanted to say why he pummeled her with questions. Tianna adjusted herself and pulled her tousled air-dried hair over her shoulder.

"Tell me."

"My father left us a long time ago, and I vowed never to be like him. I wanted a child of my own to feel loved and wanted. The woman I was dating at the time knew this. I liked her, and she pretended to love me." Tianna shifted uncomfortably at his admission. Gregory responded with another kiss.

"She pretended to be pregnant shortly after we purchased the brownstone. That's why I asked her to marry me. She lied about being pregnant. I found her secretly discarding her feminine products in the trash. She was never pregnant. She had been lying to me for months."

"Wow, that was conniving."

"She never really apologized and expected me to forgive her.. When I confronted her, she manipulated the situation, saying that we were engaged anyway. I couldn't marry a person like that, so I broke it off." Tianna looked at Gregory, who was looking down at her.

"I can understand. It wasn't just a lie; it was outright deception." Tianna turned around and held Gregory close, trying to imagine his joy and then his crushing disappointment. Now his questions made sense. He was trying to see if she would 'approve' or explain such low vibrational behavior. She would not, could not. And she is trying to marry him anyway? Tianna was sure whoever she was almost assuredly regretted it.

"Narcissism," she then said, nuzzled under his chin.

"Classic Narcissist, " he answered.

They slowly and thoroughly kissed before succumbing to sleep. The following day, she woke up by herself. She smelled coffee and turkey bacon in the air. Is this man perfect? She considered him a welcome change from her past one-sided relationships, which she ended quickly. She checked her morning breath before running to the bathroom to handle it. She was dangerously close to liking him too much.

Tianna wanted to visit a touristy place, like the African American Heritage Trail that ringed the island. It was a beautiful vacation destination. The beach was serene even with tourists; Gregory was proud of himself—he had never planned a vacation before. He took a selfie with Tianna and posted it on Instagram and Facebook at the

Japanese garden. Tianna kept saying how he made a fantastic choice. She loved the cute Gingerbread Houses, a popular attraction; the colorful, quaint Victorian houses reminded Tianna of old dollhouses. While there, Gregory's phone started vibrating and pinging with notifications so much he turned it off.

"Sorry about that."

"No problem. Work is work. Look at these cute little homes."

Gregory read about the Gingerbread Cottages and wanted Tianna to see them, her eyes danced with delight. Gregory was optimistic that the lobster dinner at Inkwell would be just as lovely as the dinner last night. He wanted to make up for missing the sunset. They arrived too late for that. By four that afternoon, they came back to the beach house, changed, and quickly headed out to Dockside for souvenirs and ordered their lobster dinner to take to the beach. Tianna wore a blue and white horizontal striped shirt with jeans, shorts, and white sandals. She was glad she packed light and researched what one wore on the Vineyard. Bringing formal or business casual clothes would not have been very comfortable. Gregory looked good in anything he wore; when he caught Tianna staring at him, he said, "My mother always told me that being handsome is a blessing and a curse." They both laughed at that one.

"Anyway," Tianna said, smiling but keeping her face away from Gregory, "let's go into one of the cute little stores." Tianna was not into vlogging, but she was finally pleased to include Gregory in her pictures. So, he took his phone out and snapped more photographs of them enjoying the day. The city of Aquinnah, located in the town of Gay Head, was built in 1857. The indigenous Wampanoag sued for the right to rename the city and won. It was now called Wampanoag.

The clay cliffs looking over the beaches made the city the most beautiful in Martha's Vineyard. It was understandable that they wanted to reclaim the land. He took most of his pictures there, another quite beautiful place. Sometimes Tianna would ramble on, and Gregory would listen; it was a welcome change from work where her patients did all the talking and Tianna just listened. She was not Dr. Tianna McQueen. She was just Tianna or Tee, no titles. They held hands and listened to the ocean meet the shoreline. The sun shimmered on the water. Gregory checked the time; if they wanted to make it to Oak Bluffs beach for dinner, they had better hurry before they didn't have a place to sit.

It was "a thing" to eat a lobster dinner near sunset at Oak Bluffs beach; the beach had sun worshippers sitting waiting for the sun to go down. Since the weekend started with dinner on Inkwell beach, it made sense that it ended with dinner on Oak Bluffs beach. Tianna took off her sandals and walked back to the car. It was the best time, hands down. She could not wait to tell Janiyah and thank her coworker for reconnecting her with Gregory. Back at the beach house mansion, Tianna changed to swim in the pool, before getting into the hot tub. Gregory joined Tianna, massaging her shoulders.

"Tianna, you are tense. Why don't you relax?" He leaned her back into his chest. Her natural curls floated in the bubbling water. His hands took her away again. She began to think with a relaxing sigh that maybe she could get used to his touch and his presence. However, it was only their first weekend; she still had to see and keep her eyes on him. Although their time together was needed and, in some ways, long overdue, Tianna was ready to get to work and implement some of the ideas she had for her office.

As Tianna and Gregory left Martha's Vineyard, heading back to their daily lives and work routines, Tianna felt the timing was right to bring up an idea that had been on her mind. She suggested they consider organizing counseling sessions specifically for the Black community—a few drop-in slots each month that would offer support to those who might not typically reach out for help. She explained that it could be not only a powerful way to give back but also excellent public relations for the company, creating a bridge to a marginalized group that often feels overlooked.

Gregory nodded thoughtfully as he listened to her proposal, a smile spreading across his face. "That sounds like a great idea," he said, genuinely impressed by her thoughtfulness. "It's definitely something we should look into." As they continued driving, Gregory's phone buzzed repeatedly with incoming notifications, breaking the moment. After a while, he turned to Tianna with a hint of amusement in his eyes.

"Looks like everyone wants to know about you," he said, his voice warm with affection. "Even my mom's been asking questions since I put our picture up." He handed his phone to Tianna, letting her see what had caught everyone's attention.

As Tianna looked through his phone, she saw a series of photos he had posted from their weekend trip—pictures of them together, their smiles glowing against the backdrop of the Vineyard's breathtaking scenery. There were candid shots of them laughing, walking along the shoreline, and even a few of Tianna admiring the view. The images radiated a sense of joy and togetherness that made her heart swell.

"Wow," Tianna said softly, feeling both touched and a little shy. "You really didn't hold back, did you?"

Gregory shrugged with a grin. "I wanted to share what a great weekend we had and how lucky I am to have you in my life." Tianna couldn't help but smile back, grateful for the way their lives seemed to be weaving together, one beautiful moment at a time.

Chapter FIFTEEN

Lillian McQueen sat at the edge of her bed, staring out the window into the late afternoon sky. The confrontation with Tianna had left her feeling hollow, as if the world she had so carefully constructed had crumbled to dust. For years, she had carried the weight of her decisions, believing she was protecting her family, but now she realized that the secrets she'd kept were like cracks in their foundation, spreading until everything shattered.

Tianna quietly entered the small kitchen through the back door, her mind swirling with thoughts. She longed to talk to her mother, but before they could speak, she needed to decide how they would communicate—whether through words of anger or something more peaceful. Whatever happened, she knew the important thing was to begin the healing process for both of them. She almost changed her mind before she left New York, but she was already on the northbound train.

Tianna stared at the blank page in front of her, her pen hovering over the paper. She had been staring at it for minutes, her mind swirling with a thousand thoughts, but none of them seemed right. The weight of the task before her—of trying to connect with her mother—felt like an insurmountable mountain. Yet, somehow, she needed to try. For both of their sakes.

She had spent years in therapy, not just as a professional but also as a patient. In her line of work, Tianna often guided others through exercises meant to break down walls, encourage communication, and promote healing. It was an approach she had used countless times with her patients, and now, perhaps it was time to apply it to herself. To her own broken relationship with her mother.

She could feel the familiar pang of uncertainty stir in her chest. Was this a good idea? Could she really share her feelings with her mother? The thought of it made her stomach tighten, but deep down, she knew she had to try. The distance between them had been growing for years, and no matter how painful, no matter how hard it felt, something had to change.

Tianna walked to her small kitchen and pulled out two clean notebooks. She set them down on the table and grabbed two pens, one for herself and one for her mother. There were no professional whiteboards, no calming pictures on the wall to ease the discomfort. Just a cluttered kitchen with peeling paint and chipped mugs in the cupboard.

It was raw. It was real. And it had to be enough.

Her mother had agreed to this, reluctantly, when Tianna suggested it during their last conversation. Lillian had been quiet, hesitant, but she had ultimately agreed, unsure of what else to do. Their history was filled with pain, lies, and unresolved anger, but maybe—just maybe—this exercise could be a way for them to start speaking again. To really hear each other for once.

Tianna took a deep breath and wrote down the first thing that came to her mind in the notebook:

"I've spent most of my life trying to understand you, and I still don't know who you really are."

Tianna paused, reading her mother's entry, rereading the second line: "I feel like I've always been your secret—someone you didn't want to acknowledge, someone you kept in the background of your life."

Her mother entered the kitchen a few moments later, hesitant but determined. Lillian sat down at the table across from Tianna, looking at the two notebooks, then at her daughter. Her eyes were tired, worn, like she hadn't slept in days, even though Tianna knew that wasn't the case. Her face was pale, but her resolve seemed firm. This was her chance—her last chance, perhaps—to fix things with Tianna. To make things right, even if it was only in small steps.

They exchanged a glance, a long, wordless moment where neither of them knew where to begin. Finally, Tianna pushed the notebook and pen across the table toward her mother. Lillian hesitated, then picked up the pen, gripping it tightly in her hand. She began to write, her movements slow, deliberate.

Tianna could feel her mother's gaze on her as she wrote. The silence was thick, suffocating. Tianna could almost hear her mother's internal struggle, the years of regret and unspoken words that had been buried deep inside her. After what felt like an eternity, Lillian set the pen down and slid the notebook across the table.

Tianna glanced at the page. It was different from what she had expected—no excuses, no defenses. Lillian had written:

"I never meant to hurt you, Tianna. I was just trying to survive. I thought I was doing what was best, even if it was wrong. I don't know how to fix it, but I want to try."

They sat in silence for a moment, the weight of the exchange settling over them. It wasn't perfect. It wasn't everything, but it was real. Tianna picked up her own notebook and wrote one more thing, something she hadn't expected to say:

"I forgive you, but I need you to understand that forgiveness takes time. I can't just erase the past."

She slid the notebook back to her mother, watching as Lillian read the words. Lillian blinked, and for the first time in a long while, her eyes softened with something resembling vulnerability.

After a few more moments of silence, they did something unexpected. They swapped notebooks.

Reading her mother's words—honest and unfiltered—was a jolt of reality for Tianna. Lillian wasn't perfect. She wasn't the woman Tianna had once hoped she would be. But she was trying. And that, in itself, was something. They sat there for a while, absorbing what had been said, before deciding to move on to the next step of the exercise.

They both tore out the pages and, without a word, ripped them into pieces. It was symbolic, a way to let go of the past. The hurt, the disappointment, the anger—it was time to release it, to burn it away. And that's what they did.

Finally, they took their pens again and wrote affirming words about each other—things they admired, things they had never said aloud. They wrote affirmations of forgiveness, of hope, of possibility.

Tianna wrote:

"I see you're trying, and that means something to me. You're not the person you were, and I want to believe in who you're becoming."

Her mother wrote:

"You are strong, Tianna. You have always been stronger than I realized. I'm proud of you, even if I've never said it enough."

It was a small step, but it was a start.

Lillian's face crumpled with relief and regret all at once. They sat there in silence for a moment, letting the weight of the past lift just a little. Lillian reached into her pocket and pulled out a small, folded piece of paper. "I wrote down the lies I've told myself, the ones I told you. I wanted to tear them up together, if you're willing."

As they tore the paper, Lillian said, "This isn't just about me being sorry, Tianna. It's about me finally facing what I've done and choosing to be better. For you, and for me."

Tianna looked at her mother, the tightness in her chest loosening just a little. "I can't promise that everything will be okay right away," she said. "But I'm willing to give us a chance. To try to rebuild what we lost."

Lillian nodded, a soft smile spreading across her face despite the tears. "Thank you," she whispered. "That's all I want for our family."

They stood up, and Lillian hesitated for a moment before reaching out to pull Tianna into a hug. It was tentative at first, but then Tianna wrapped her arms around her mother tightly, feeling the warmth and sincerity in that embrace. It was the first time in a long while that they held each other not just as mother and daughter, but as two women ready to heal together.

As they pulled apart, Tianna took a deep breath and said, "We should do something together—a fresh start. Maybe plant a tree in the garden? Something to remind us that we can grow from this."

Lillian's eyes lit up, the hint of a smile breaking through her tear-streaked face. "I'd like that," she said. "A new beginning."

They walked to the garden in the fading light of the afternoon, finding a spot to plant the small sapling they had decided would symbolize their journey. As they dug into the soil, their hands working side by side, it felt like they were planting more than just a tree. They were planting hope, a promise that the future could be different.

As the last bit of earth was patted down around the sapling, they stood back, looking at their work. The garden was still, the sky beginning to turn the colors of dusk. "Mom," Tianna said quietly, "I'm not ready to forget everything that happened, but I am ready to move forward. I just need you to be honest with me from now on. No more lies."

Lillian nodded, her tears falling freely now. "I'll be here when you're ready," she said, her voice small but full of sincerity. "I'll spend the rest of my life trying to make up for what I've done."

Tianna took a deep breath, her emotions still raw. She couldn't give her mother what she wanted—not yet. But there was a small flicker of hope, a belief that one day, they could find their way back to each other.

Without another word, Tianna turned and walked toward the door. As she left, Lillian remained seated, staring into the half-empty coffee cup in front of her, realizing the damage was done. But she held onto the hope that, in time, her daughter might find it in her heart to heal—and maybe, one day, forgive.

They stood there together, the newly planted tree between them, its branches reaching toward the sky. It was a symbol of their past, their pain, and their hope for a future that would be built on honesty and love.

With her heart entangled in new feelings, she felt justified in her anger towards Lillian, who seemed to be oblivious to her daughter's emotional turmoil. She didn't want to be reminded of the complications that lingered in her family, especially when her heart was leaning towards something fresh and hopeful.

The combination of hunches and leads had not yielded substantial progress in the investigation. Sergeant Lee, who had been a steady presence in the precinct for years, was retiring at the end of the year, and there was an unspoken urgency in the air. His impending departure weighed heavily on the department, and Garcia felt the pressure mounting. It was imperative to make significant strides before Lee left, but the pieces just weren't falling into place.

Just then, her phone buzzed, interrupting her thoughts. It was a message from Gregory, lighthearted and full of warmth. It reminded her of what she wanted to hold on to—the excitement, the passion, and the joy of a new relationship. In that moment, she decided she would prioritize her happiness over her mother's mounting desperation. But as the days turned into weeks, she couldn't shake the nagging feeling that ignoring Lillian might have consequences far beyond her immediate frustration.

Janiyah wanted to call Detective Garcia; she could not decide if she had information or just found him cute.

"Yeah, we've been piecing that together. It turns out Victor was still drinking the night of the accident. We've got witnesses placing him there, and your father's statement would help confirm it."

"My dad mentioned that night. He said Victor was completely wasted when he saw him. But I thought he got clean?"

"He did, eventually. The community center held substance abuse meetings and that helped him to get sober. He volunteered there and stuck with the AA meetings afterward, but that night… The night of the accident, Victor fell off the wagon. He was drunk when it happened."

Detective Garcia gave up trying to have a personal conversation and let Janiyah rant on speaker phone. Five minutes in, Lee made a face. Garcia took her off speaker again.

Sgt. Lee chimes in once again. "I've got all of this documented. I want to close this case before my retirement. It's been hanging over me for too long. If I can just tie up these loose ends, I can go out knowing it's finished. That's where your father's statement comes in, Janiyah. We need him to officially write down what he saw at the pool hall. It'll help us put the final pieces together."

Janiyah caught the background conversation. "Detective Garcia, you told me earlier that this case would make Lee look good. Is that what this is about?" Garcia rubbed his goatee, then shrugged. "It's not just about that, Janiyah. We want to bring closure to Tianna's family, but let's be real—solving a case this old before a retirement party? It doesn't hurt."

"Right… so my father's statement is important. I get it. What exactly do you need from him?"

Garcia shifted in his seat. He felt grilled but maintained his composure. "He just needs to describe what he saw and heard that night. Specifically, if he can confirm that Victor was drinking heavily and if he remembers any details about his behavior. We already know Victor was driving drunk, but any additional information from someone who knew him, like your father, helps us build the case. Once we get his statement, we'll talk to Victor again. And we'll be able to bring some resolution to the families involved.".

"My dad's memory isn't what it used to be. He might not remember every detail."

Garcia, ever the diplomat, volunteered, "It's okay if it's not perfect. We just need whatever he can recall. Even if it's fragments—times, places, anything like that. It all helps paint a clearer picture of what happened."

"Okay… I'll talk to him. But this has to be about more than just your retirement party, detective. I want justice for Tianna's father. He deserves that closure." Janiyah breathed a sigh of relief.

Sargent Lee's deep sigh said a lot without saying a word. Garcia stifled a chuckle. "It is about justice, Janiyah. We've been working on this case for years. We wouldn't be pushing so hard if we didn't think it would help. Believe me, I want this resolved as much as you do. Look, Janiyah, this is tough for all of us. We're trying to piece together what happened that night so that families can finally heal. Victor's role in all of this is still unclear, but with your father's help, we'll know for sure. And once we do, we can move forward with the investigation and bring some closure to everyone affected."

Janiyah didn't care that she was being pushy, sometimes it was the pushy people that had gotten results. "I'll talk to him. I'll get his statement, but I want updates. I don't want to be left in the dark anymore. Too much time has passed for this to stay unresolved."

"You have my word. We'll keep you updated every step of the way. Once your father's statement is in, we'll be reviewing everything again and interviewing Victor as well.

"And if Victor was responsible, I want him held accountable. He can't just walk away from this. He killed someone's kid," Janiyah added vehemently.

"We are looking into everything. If Victor's actions that night caused harm, we'll make sure he answers for it. You have our commitment to that. Lee was looking at Garcia suspiciously. This was a case, not a Love Connection, so he took control of the conversation.

Sitting back, pensively. "We've got the information now. It's about pulling it together—your father's account, the AA meetings, the community center. We'll find out what happened, Janiyah. And we'll make sure this case is finally closed the right way. Thanks for calling again." He said then rolled his eyes. "We will take it from here. Bye, now"

"Bye," Janiyah said then hung up. Only to call back to ask another question.

"A real *Aretha Christie*. This is our case. The last thing I need is a civilian solving my old case before my retirement," Lee interjected.

"We won't. We're on it."

Garcia ends the call with Janiyah. Lee looked at him, "So whatcha got?"

"We may have another lead," Detective Garcia said. A young drug addicted youth, Jaheim told me last night that he and I quote: Know somebody, that know somebody that know somebody possibly is attached to that hit in run of Richie.

The sergeant wanted the information to be definitive and looked skeptical at his subordinate.

"Possibly? Did he mention Victor?"

"How accurate? Not sure. No. he did not mention Victor. But I gave him that day's lunch money. Garcia raised his hands in a 'I don't know' gesture."

"Keep me posted."

Tianna gave in to her thoughts about Gregory. She thought about him more than she wanted to admit. He stayed on her mind when he wasn't around. She liked him more than she previously thought. She should be focusing on her demanding work deadlines. Her clinic was one of the test sites for a new psychotic drug, and the number of patients had doubled. Her work week consumed most of her free time. She barely had time to walk the two blocks to Starbucks.

After a long day, Tianna made a wheat pita hummus and boiled egg sandwich. Engrossed in writing her summaries, she didn't notice her phone ringing. It was Gregory. She wanted to call him three days ago but waited, not wanting to disturb his schedule.

"Hey, stranger," he said, his deep voice tickling her spine and warming her with memories of their lovemaking last week.

"Hey, how are you?" she asked, though she wanted to say she missed him.

"It's been almost two weeks since we hung out. Let's not let this slip into something tawdry." Tianna giggled like a schoolgirl.

“I want to see you more,” Gregory admitted. He liked her and didn’t want to lie about it.

“I missed you,” Tianna admitted. “But I was busy with work.”

“Oh, so you missed me,” he said. “Well, I missed you too. Now what?”

“Let’s plan to go out. How about Pelham Park on Sunday?”

“Okay, it’s a date.” Tianna enjoyed his company, both indoors and outdoors. They talked about everything: politics, science, art, celebrity gossip, dreams, aspirations, goals. Gregory believed in setting new goals every year, and she liked that. Self-improvement was a lifelong pursuit for her, and it was nice to find someone who agreed.

Her phone beeped. “Gregory, can I call you later? My mother is calling.”

“Tianna, hi. Honey, are you busy? I hope not. Next weekend, I have some free time and would like to visit.”

“Sure, Mom,” Tianna replied, unsure how her schedule would accommodate her mother’s visit. She had never been to New York and wanted to plan the visit.

“Mom, let me rearrange my schedule and call you back on Tuesday.”

The next morning, Tianna started her busy day. "Good morning, Ms. McQueen. Would you like coffee or tea?" Mallory Green, the office secretary, asked.

"I'll take coffee, thanks. A little cream, two sugars."

Tianna picked up her mail from Mallory, who handled calls for seven clinicians. Annoyingly, some could be rude to her. No sooner had Tianna sat down than Mallory was on the intercom.

"You have a call on line three, Dr. McQueen."

On her rare day off, Tianna cleaned her home from top to bottom. She was in the process of buying the entire brownstone, not just her apartment. Lillian's stock and dividends from profit-sharing helped cover most of her student loans for graduate school and her Ph.D. The rest of her loan was fifty-nine thousand, which she was paying off. Buying the building at her full salary seemed perfect since her residential training would be over the following year. She was almost ready for the monumental deposit.

Mrs. Hart, the current owner, insisted that Florida was the ideal place to be year-round. "Tianna, close your eyes and picture green grass and trees everywhere, palm trees swaying in the breeze, and the intoxicating aroma of fresh limes and ripe mangos. Go to your happy place," she encouraged with a smile.

Tianna nodded but replied, "I see it." However, her mind wandered to the vibrant hustle of New York. Harlem was prime real estate, and she envisioned herself buying property in the city that never sleeps, where opportunities thrived amid the chaos. "But what about the house in Brockton?" she pressed, a hint of uncertainty in her voice.

"I will be moving in a few months, Tianna. With your father in the hospital. You can have the house then, after your paperwork is processed." Meanwhile, Lillian was ending her call and added, "Mrs. Hart, it sounds beautiful. When do you see yourself moving?" As she hung up, the allure of Mrs. Hart's sunny Florida dream mingled with Tianna's yearning for the bustling streets of Harlem, showcasing the classic struggle between serenity and ambition in their decisions about home. The question lingered in the air—where would each choose to establish their roots? Her mother made it clear which one she would choose.

Tianna was excited about possibly owning a brownstone in Harlem, like an official New Yorker. She hoped her mother would be proud and would not mind. She did not see herself in Florida. Gregory of course would be happy if she stayed in New York. Cleaning her apartment, Tianna spoke positivity into existence, envisioning owning the entire building. Her spirit was unsettled as she thought about her mother. They had a terrible relationship and she was determined to fix it, but didn't know how. Years of unkind words had strained their bond.

Tianna picked up her cell phone and called her mother. “Hello, Mom, it’s me. How are you? I haven’t spoken to you in a while. It’s so good to hear your voice. How have you been?”

“I’m good. Sleeping better lately. How is everything? Your father hasn’t been feeling well. He’s moving slower and needs help around the house. I have a lady check on him when I’m not home. Even though I stopped working as a security guard, I still work from 9:00 to 5:00 at the law office, Monday through Friday. The bills don’t stop coming, baby girl. I still have to work.”

Her mother described her day with her father in detail, and Tianna felt guilty she couldn't be more help. She had a full-time job to pay for things her mother needed assistance with—the old crumbling house, the new condo in Florida, and a sick spouse. Her mother needed a break but had to work extra hours. Tianna's internship was almost over, and once she had a firmer footing in her company, she could make more adjustments to her schedule. Ralph's health had deteriorated due to alcohol, an elephant in the room neither wanted to mention.

Gregory was texting about the new movie that was out ‘Zombie and the Maiden.’ Tianna promised to visit soon. And she needed to call him back. He had a knack for making plans. As the calendar flipped to Friday, he saw an opportunity to spend quality time with Tianna. He quickly texted her, suggesting they catch a movie that evening. "I've got tickets to that new romantic comedy you mentioned!" he wrote, hoping to spark her enthusiasm. The thought of watching a light-hearted film and enjoying popcorn together brought a smile to Tianna's face, momentarily easing the heaviness weighing on her heart.

As the time drew near, Tianna dressed carefully, wanting to look her best for her date. She picked out a comfortable yet stylish outfit, glancing in the mirror to check her reflection. But beneath the surface of her excitement, guilt lurked like a shadow. Her thoughts drifted to her father, gravely ill, and her mother, who was struggling to manage everything on her own. She had promised to help, yet here she was, preparing for a night out instead of being by her family's side.

When the doorbell rang, Tianna took a deep breath and opened the door to find Gregory grinning, holding a small bouquet of flowers. "For my favorite girl," he said, presenting them with a flourish. The gesture warmed her heart, but as they headed out to the car, the knot of guilt tightened in her stomach.

"Handsome and punctual, I like it."

She enjoyed the date but her father was lingering in the back of her mind. Between work, Gregory and her parents Tianna's hands were full.

SIXTEEN

One case was giving Tianna trouble. She didn't like it. The more she thought about that specific case, the more convinced she was that she was out of her league. The client was outsmarting her, and she knew it. The problem was he was a liar, plain and simple. He needed to be evaluated to determine his competency to stand trial for attacking the elderly at Chelsea Piers. He would redirect their conversations, going completely off-topic. It was a court-mandated session, and if it were inconclusive, a lunatic could be running loose, attacking older adults without a proper diagnosis. And it was all an act.

Patient A1, as he was called on the chart, exaggerated his already awkward personality: speaking about himself in the third person or doing repetitive actions like tapping his ears ten times within the hour-long session. He avoided questions about his upbringing or past. The session would start with where he lived as a child and gradually turn to the many planets in space. Dr. McQueen was baffled, and after three sessions, she wanted to pawn him off on a more experienced clinician. Dr. Tianna knew she had to service this lunatic. She knew bullshit when she heard it. It was going to be a long week.

"Hey, what a nice-looking set of parents you have."

Tianna bristled. Her clients usually sat down throughout the session. The strange man from the mental hospital was nosy, but she asked, "Simon, please sit down."

"That's a nice picture. Are these your parents?"

"Umm, yes, they are. I was receiving my doctorate, she cautiously added." The mistake in telling her client was like stubbing her toe in the dark.

"Are you an only child?" he asked. Tianna did not answer, but her face told the story.

"How long ago did they pass?"

"Oh, did I say if I had a brother or sister? I don't think I mentioned…."

"It's okay. I'm good at guessing things." Tianna did not like where their conversation was heading. He was crossing the patient to the therapist line. And his questions felt like some weird manipulation.

"Well, this time, you're mistaken," she said with a smirk. "And, we are out of time."

She made sure to document the entire session. Later that evening, she relayed her day to Gregory.

"Nope. I don't like this, Tianna. Be careful. He sounds dangerous."

"That's what I said. I decided to pass on this 'opportunity.' He's crazy and sneaky as hell, off the record, of course."

"Of course," he said with a smirk.

"Tianna, you don't have to worry about me repeating anything you tell me or worry about me turning it into a segment for my radio station. Besides, I talk sexy for the women and make some dudes listen to the after-hours show. Who knows, maybe they imitate me, sometimes. This sexy deep voice is my moneymaker, and that's it."

"Gregory, do you like your job, or are you just used to the fame that comes with it? You told me that ladies love it." He thought briefly about what she was saying. He couldn't remember a time when he didn't want to be on the radio, but he also wanted to use his platform for something more than just good music.

"Well, I did want to be a gospel singer," he answered.

"You did? What made you change your mind?"

"Thou shall not fornicate. I don't think I could have kept that promise, and with so many headhunters in the pews, the temptation would have come, and I would have fallen."

"Headhunters?"

"You know, headhunters." He looked down at the crotch of his pants. Tianna gave him a look. "What?" he asked, shrugging. "A man should know his limitations," he said, laughing. Tianna's disapproving look made him laugh harder. "A tasteless joke, I know. But you've seen women looking for husbands and lovers instead of coming to church for Jesus. I would have been a hypocrite, so why bother, right?"

"Ooh, I see," Tianna said after a while. She could not focus on Gregory's light testing. Her mind was still on her newest case. The lawyers for both sides needed a summary of her findings, and she didn't have one yet; it was too soon. Looking down at her watch, she said, "It's getting late, and I have two reports to write tonight," which meant no wine or coffee in the morning type-of dates. Gregory was disappointed. He was looking forward to a repeat of what they had done on Martha's Vineyard; it would be missing the beautiful beach house and the island, but he was willing to try. The night was still young, but naturally, it was at her discretion. He made his way to her door with heavy feet and swollen body parts.

He kissed her gently on the mouth and took the train further uptown. He was amazed that they would even see each other again. When they were in their small world, they were in a city of at least eight million other people and at least ninety-five thousand in Brockton, Massachusetts. And only within the company of each other was it calm, peaceful and kind of complete.

Tianna cleared away the Chinese takeout and cleaned her kitchen, she regretted sending Gregory home. She had the creeps just thinking about Simon (Patient A1) Guthery. She got the niggling feeling that he was indeed crazy, but not criminally insane, crazy—more like 'I am more intelligent than you will ever be' crazy. So, she buckled down to start a summary of their interaction. She wouldn't be able to conclude from visits, but he had the creep gauge on lock so far.

As soon as Gregory reached home, he called Tianna to check on her. He dialed her number and didn't reach her on the first try. He took his lukewarm shower and headed to bed. He called once more, getting her; she was out of breath.

"Hello," she said on the other end, breathing deeply.

"What's wrong? Are you okay?"

"I ran for the phone. I figured it was you. I miss you already," Tianna admitted, surprising herself. "I mean, I don't want you to worry." She snuggled deeply into warm covers. They smelled like him. After allowing herself ten minutes, she was up again. There was work to do.

"Oh. Okay, cool. I just wanted to call. That strange little client of yours crossed my mind. I just want to make sure the little dude doesn't start lurking or anything. I mean, I can come over and spend a few nights..."

"Nice try, but no. I have work to do." Tianna felt better just hearing his voice. "Thank you for the invitation, though. I think I like having you around the place."

"No problem," Gregory replied, though he sounded disappointed. They had time, but that time was not now, not when she had a deadline for an evaluation. Tianna stayed up that night, going through past case studies of criminals pretending to be insane to avoid full responsibility for their actions. On one hand, she could make a mistake, and a young man could get sentenced as a regular inmate, or that same man could be placed in a hospital for a short time other than prison and be released to commit the same crime. Elder abuse ranges from one to seven years, depending on the severity.

Tianna's cases had been lightweight until Patient A1, and it was essential to show she was the right pick for her position. So as much as she wanted the company, she couldn't risk it. His intake page read: Patient A117 has a history of violent outbursts in public. Not on any medication. The second meeting was very much like the first.

The days blurred into a steady stream of patients confiding familiar woes: unfulfillment, feeling undervalued by spouses, or being dismissed by supervisors. Between appointments, Tianna made time for coffee with Gregory, Sabrina, or her new co-worker, Maxine. Maxine, however, was different. Craving connection but unable to maintain it, she clung to gossip and negativity, leaving Tianna drained after every interaction. Tianna had grown weary of Maxine's catty remarks and her penchant for soul-sucking conversations. Still, she had invited her over once more, hoping to find some common ground—or at least keep the peace.

“Let’s do brunch soon,” Tianna said, forcing a smile as she stretched and stood. Air kisses were exchanged before Maxine, with her expensive bag slung over her shoulder, finally left. The door barely clicked shut before Tianna exhaled deeply, muttering, “I need to burn some sage.”

The room felt heavy, as if Maxine's energy had seeped into the walls. Tianna rummaged through her cabinets, finding the small bundle of sage she’d forgotten about. She lit it, pacing the room with a mix of frustration and resolve. Maxine’s inconsistent friendship had reached its limit. Tianna didn’t have the time—or the mental space—to keep pretending. Minutes later, a loud crash snapped her out of her thoughts. Her coffee had toppled, taking her laptop with it. Staring at the cracked screen, she groaned. Maybe she should’ve burned the sage longer. Gregory called to check on her, but the stressed tone in her voice left him asking, "Rough day?"

"I am imploding. I just broke my computer, and it is 10 pm; I still have so much to do."

"Don’t panic. I got you."

"What..."

"Supa man is on the way."

"You are at work, so…"

"Prerecorded means? We tape shows just for these types of situations." Gregory had his assistant pick up her brand-new computer from Best Buy, which closes at midnight, so she needed it ASAP.

Tianna was surprised when a courier brought her new computer to her. Reasons why she liked him—he was thoughtful, she thought, and slightly distracted played with the top button of her pajamas as she thought about Gregory. With a deep breath, Tianna buckled down to start the summary form for Patient A1. It was two when she stopped researching and gathering her notes. Exhausted, she placed the new computer and noted that they would have to wait in the morning.

There were not many women psychologists where she worked, a whole two percent at the office. It was a white male-dominated profession, so Dr. Tianna McQueen wanted to work even more complex than the unspoken unwritten black tax.

Black professionals had to work harder than their white counterparts for respect or equal pay. Since then, the term has been reprocessed and packaged to mean something else; it now means black professionals that carry the financial weight of the entire family. Tianna scoffed at the new meaning of the term. Black tax had to be explained to close friends that had no idea what it was to be a black person in this country, affluent, poor, well-known or not. Prejudices aside, only Tianna was focused on professionalism and common respect at the workplace, everything less was not helpful in their line of work.

Chapter SEVENTEEN

Dr. McQueen filled out the standard evaluation form and then her Simon or Patient A1 summary.

Summary Case #43219A PatientA117

Placing a recorder to her lips she evaluated the meeting with her client. Notated her observations. Patient A117, Simon Guthery, seems to have a particular hostility towards older women. He needs further evaluation at a participating facility. At present, he poses a danger to the community and requires counseling. A brief stay at an institution is preferred over mandatory sentencing for elder abuse. Although his hallucinations sometimes seem exaggerated, his clarity and questions often appear as deliberate attacks. This is my endnote to the form already filled out. Her cellphone rang as she continued writing her side notes on her new patient..

"Dr. McQueen?" It was Mallory, the office secretary. She rarely called anyone at home unless it was necessary.

"Hello, Mallory. Is everything okay at the office?"

"Yes, Dr. Swartz wants you to give him a call. It's about one of your patients."

Tianna was afraid this was going to happen. She did not want to lose any clients after working with them. She was still proving herself at the clinic.

"Hello, Dr. Swartz," Tianna said, trying to sound composed. He was one of the top doctors at the clinic; however, he constantly confused Tianna with the secretaries at work. Stepping into his office were leather-bound books graced mahogany and lacquered shelves. She sat down for the update of PatientA117.

"Oh yes, Tianna—Dr. McQueen, I mean. We have an update on your patient Simon uhhh, A117. He has been arrested again. It took some time but he has been charged with menacing an ex-girlfriend and her elderly mother. They are the reason he was attacking the older women in Chelsea, Manhattan. It was because the ex-girlfriend broke up with him, and her mother wanted her to. He lied about his income, and the family did not want the daughter involved with him any longer. So, he is being arrested for elder abuse and additional charges of menacing and harassing. I appreciate the work you were doing with him. Thank you so much. But I want you to submit a summary, and you can discard the patient evaluation. He's being officially charged today."

He was no longer her responsibility and off the streets, Tianna thought, and it felt good to be recognized in even a small way at work. The trust and responsibilities given to her with her clients seemed to make up for the hectic work schedule. It was a blessing that Simon was off the streets, but Tianna would rather stick to the bored narcissistic clients she had—no more Simons. She called Gregory right away, knowing he would be relieved.

Tianna sat in her office, it was small with a sliver of a window, fading light streamed in, it was late afternoon. Her last client should be at the clinic within the hour. Tianna's mother had also been trying to reach her. She left two messages on her cellphone and three at work. Tianna knew it had to do with her father. She wasn't sure she was ready to hear any bad news, not after finishing her week strong. She wanted to ride that wave of accomplishment for a while. Usually, when her mother called, it was not good news.

"Thanks, Mallory." Switching over to line three, she took a deep breath, held it then released it.

"Hello… hello?"

"Hello, mom," Tianna answered reluctantly. She did not want to have any conversation that would put her in an emotional headspace. She needed to be clear for her clients.

"Mom, why didn't you go to the hospital with dad?"

"Because I knew he would be okay. So, I waited till the morning."

"Mom, the morning? Really. I was worried about him; I could hardly sleep. Is he feeling better?"

"Yes, he is, for now."

"For now?"

"I hate to break it to you, Tianna. This is what alcoholism is."

"What? Mom, what are you saying?"

"Your father has a drinking problem, and it was there way before your brother passed. First it was just a beer then two, then a six pack all to relax. Now it is much much more than that. Haven't you noticed all these years?"

"Mom, I am at work. I can't have this type of conversation here. And I am expecting a client."

Tianna knew it but did not want to admit it. Her father loved her so much and took care of her. He was her hero, and she did not want to confront his flaws.

"Now, Tee, I know you are at work, so I won't hold you. But I want to call you later after work to talk. Or give your father a call."

"Okay, mom, let's talk later." It was too much to admit or digest. She did not want to think about family issues at work.

Later that night Tianna held the recorder in her hand as she paced the floor later in her apartment.

"Any reaction to anxiety or stress exhibiting itself can be expressed through dysregulated behaviors. Interesting start now what?" she said to herself. She turned it off again. Where was this going? She sounded stiff and off in her own ears. Tianna lost her train of thought and put the device down on the table. She had another thesis to write and was nervous about her delivery—forty pages in, and she had to rewrite so much of it.

Would it be good enough? Will it make sense? Does it flow? Tianna questioned herself as she adjusted the curtains. Brain fog, she thought—it was time for a break. She pivoted towards her tiny refrigerator. The newest Ben and Jerry's ice cream was calling her name, but she knew that was stress eating; if she was going to nibble on something, it should be a proper meal. A pepper jack cheese, a slice or two of turkey bacon and tomato sandwich on wheat bread hit the spot. It was eight PM when she wiped off her tiny table. The rent in New York was expensive and steadily climbing. She hoped to work hard enough to own property in the city or surrounding areas.

Although Tianna had studied for her doctorate, she was nervous to present her oral presentation in clinical psychology, so she occasionally purchased books with the new twenty-first-century self-help mantra: YOU ARE ENOUGH. She tried to apply what she learned in school to her own life but was unsure if she was effective enough to judge her own progress. She would pull out books and read upon hypothetical scenarios close to her current situations.

Yet she knew she could not diagnose or treat herself, which is why other clinical professionals seek help from their colleagues.

Simply put, doctors saw other doctors. Tianna was reminded of something her mother always told her: "If you want it bad enough, then you will have it." Tianna felt re-energized and began using the discarded recorder and typing her thoughts again. She felt more self-assured and determined to finish her self-mandated three hours. Since she would be shadowing her first week at the new clinic, she needed to be tested. Never had Dr. Tianna been pushed so much until she had her first barking client.

She knew it was official, that she was legit. "Mr. Tanner, can you tell me how barking in public makes you feel?" It was an absurd question for a man who chose to bark and embarrass his wife instead of confronting her rudeness.

"I feel released and set free from the constraints of society. It has no hold on me." He was utterly convinced that he was doing something very ordinary, like taking out the trash or reading the morning paper.

"How do you think your wife feels when you bark in public? Is she embarrassed? Do you like it when she is embarrassed?"

"I do not care. It is my body. Why can't I do what I want with my body? She does what she wants with hers."

"What do you mean? Can you elaborate?"

"She emasculates me sometimes in public. She cuts me down in front of my friends." Mr. Tanner sought to humiliate himself first because of her undercutting him. He found her negative attitude about him annoying and, of course, blamed her for everything wrong with his career and their lackluster love life. As Tianna recommended a great divorce attorney, Dr. McQueen encouraged Ned Tanner and his wife to seek counseling separately and together.

After a few sessions' improvements, it took a while, but allowing Mr. Tanner to explore his defeatism and dejectedness, he could slowly stop. And without visualizing that his wife was choking to death on a miniature hotdog as he gleefully told his therapist.

Through role-playing, Dr. Tianna McQueen helped his wife understand her husband. It did not happen overnight, but her supervisor began to see her commitment to her patients in several months. She has been offered a full-time position at a clinic on the westside of Manhattan. She did not have an office with a view, but Tianna was proud of herself. After Mr. Tanner, the clients ranged from mildly displeased with their lives to borderline suicidal, kinky, or just bored and needing to talk. After a while, she wanted to do more within underserved communities. Maxine called to confer over the presentation at the convention. Tianna could have kicked herself when she agreed to let her come over. And then thought about sharing about underserved communities was a bad idea.

"So, you are leaving the office to advise ear hustlers, huh?"

"Not tomorrow—hell, maybe not this year or next year, but it is something I think about. Pretty much, I want to feel useful, like really.

I no longer want to cater to wealthy weirdos who want their counselors to co-sign their crazy."

"So when will this happen?" Maxine asked. She was the Doubting Thomas friend, and a lonely person Tianna did not want to throw into the hater category. Tianna learned to be wary of oversharing anything with her. The last thing she wanted was negativity. Her mother was there for that. Mrs. Lillian McQueen cornered the market by stepping on them.

"Uhhh, I am still working on the kinks, Maxine. When I am ready to launch, I will let you know."

"Okay, sis, I see you trying to do big things."

"Yup. But Maxine, I did it, dearie. I do have four degrees," Tianna added with a wink; she could not miss an opportunity to sass her co-worker.

"So, how are things going with your new boo-thang?" Maxine kept asking about him only to give unsolicited advice. Was this how I sounded to Janiyah, Tianna wondered.

"Well," Tianna started, guarded once again. "He is okay, although we are from the same neighborhood. We are taking it slow." Tianna said that much with a straight face. Gregory left her bed to get ready for work; she missed him and found herself thinking about him when he was not in her presence.

"Work keeps him busy."

"I bet," Maxine piped in.

What does that mean? Tianna felt her temperature rising. As a specialist, she knew that conversations with frenemies were a waste of time, it was friendship without reciprocity. Tianna was generous with Maxine to a fault, hoping it would be rewarded with genuine friendship, it did not.

"Do you know something I don't?"

"No, sis, how are they? It would be best if you educated me. I don't get around like that and choose my lovers wisely." It was another jab, but Maxine had it coming.

"Please stop, Dr. Tianna. If he has a penis, he has options and knows it. There are so many lonely women out there."

Tianna knew this; she was looking at one. She then looked at her part-time friend/acquaintance/antagonist and decided not to continue the conversation.

"Girl," Tianna laughed. "Maxine, Maxine. Mind the business that is paying you. Don't you have a man? I have to get back to these clients."

She tried it. Again. Tianna did not badger her about the midget she dated. Maxine tried to offer her rebuttal, only to be cut off. Her father called it jaw-jacking, running one's mouth, and wasting other people's time. Tianna just looked at her and shook her head. She could diagnose and analyze Maxine all day, but there were more important things to do. Tianna had to submit her invoice to the clinic, those billable hours, and she almost forgot she needed to set up her schedule and availability.

"Okay," Tianna stretched long and stood up. "I have so much to do, but we need to grab brunch or something." Tianna knew that it was a hollow promise, but no one could blame her that brunch would occur on the twelfth of NEVA. With air kisses exchanged, Maxine left. Tianna blew out the air. Whew... Maxine was an energy zapper.

` Maxine had always battled with rejection and depression, struggles that seemed to cling to her, shaping the way she interacted with others. But more than that, she lacked the emotional intelligence to be anyone's friend. She couldn't pick up on the needs or feelings of others, nor did she seem to understand the basic give-and-take of a healthy relationship. Friendship, to Maxine, was a one-sided affair—a dumping ground for her complaints, insecurities, and emotional baggage. She never asked how anyone else was doing, and even if she did, it was clear she didn't truly care for the answer.

Tianna had grown tired of Maxine's catty remarks and constant need for validation. In college, she had been more patient, willing to offer advice and emotional support whenever Maxine's life spiraled into chaos. But now, Tianna no longer felt the obligation to cater to someone so stuck in self-destructive cycles. Maxine continued picking toxic, soul-sucking men who mirrored her own emotional instability, and Tianna had no energy left to play the role of savior.

These days, Tianna was in a comfortable space in her life. Gregory, her fiancé, was a source of peace and stability, and their relationship grounded her in ways that made her protective of her emotional energy. Listening to Maxine tear down her own life, over and over again, drained Tianna. She had started to dread their conversations, knowing that nothing positive or uplifting would come out of them.

After Maxine's latest visit, Tianna felt suffocated by the weight of her friend's negativity. It was the same conversation they'd had countless times before—complaints about men, work, and life in general. Maxine couldn't see how her own choices were part of the problem, and she didn't seem to care to learn. Once she left, Tianna grabbed a bundle of sage from her drawer, needing to clear the emotional heaviness that lingered in her home. She lit the sage and let the smoke drift through the air, opening the windows to let the cool breeze carry the negative energy out.

Who knows, she thought, maybe this will clear more than just the air. Maybe it would create the emotional space she needed to finally distance herself from Maxine's toxic influence. Tianna wasn't sure when their friendship had shifted from support to a drain on her spirit, but it had. And she wasn't going to let it take her down anymore.

As the sun dipped below the horizon, casting its golden glow over her living room, Tianna felt a sense of release. It wasn't her job to fix Maxine or to suffer through her friend's emotional blind spots anymore. Maxine might never understand what it means to truly be a friend, and Tianna was okay with that. She had her own peace to protect now.

"Come in, mom; why did you take a trip up here?"

"I wanted to ride the Amtrak. I have not ridden the train in so long; I thought it would bea good idea to see my only daughter. Can I treat my only daughter to dinner?"

"I was going on a date, but I can cancel. Mom, where is your overnight bag?"

"Oh, I did not bring one. I wanted to visit, but I also like sleeping in my bed. I am sure it is out of habit, and I did not bring a change of clothes."

"I know you are on this house-buying journey, and I want to help," Lillian began.

"Mom, I cannot allow you to sacrifice any of your retirement money…Dipping into your 401K has penalties."

"You are the only child I have left. Besides, after seeing you graduate, I wanted to see you own your first home. The company I worked for, Bradley & Willard, allowed their employees to participate in their group stock investments. “I made sixty thousand. With what you have left over from your grandmother’s life insurance, you could make a reasonable down payment, right?” her mother asked, beaming. As much as Tianna wanted to refuse, the idea of renovating an old brownstone stirred something warm inside her, like happy butterflies fluttering in her stomach.

Without hesitation, her mother placed the account information in her hand, her smile soft yet insistent. Tianna stared at the papers, torn between gratitude and an urge to prove she could do this on her own. Her mother had always been quick to help, but accepting felt like an admission of weakness. Still, the prospect of owning a home—a real one with history and character—was irresistible. Just then, Detective Garcia called. "We have a strong lead," he said.

He never gave up. Tianna was grateful, though she wasn’t sure if he would ever be successful. A deep sigh of relief passed through her, as if the weight of months of uncertainty had lifted, if only for a moment. Lillian almost forgot detectives were still trying to find the driver from that night. But every time they discussed the accident, a dark cloud of suspicion formed. Lillian couldn't shake the feeling that the guilty party was standing in the room with her daughter. Her eyes would linger on Tianna’s fiancé, but she never spoke of her suspicions aloud.

Tianna, on the other hand, felt a sense of peace knowing she wouldn’t have to ask or borrow from her mother, even though the help was always there. And Lillian, though relieved to avoid another conversation about her own foolishness that fateful night, found a different kind of comfort in their small shared victory. The trip hadn't been a waste after all. Handing over the savings account and going out to dinner was just as good—maybe even better. For now, they could pretend the secrets between them weren't growing larger with each passing day.

Lillian was pleasantly surprised that she and her daughter were getting along so well; this day was unheard of in the past, reasons why she did not want to bring up the past.

The next morning Det. Garcia called Lillian it was all his Sargent's doing. He made a promise to solve her dead son's case, before he retired. That is the one case he was determined to solve. Someone knew something. Why was it that no one wanted to help unless money was involved?

Tianna's phone ringing brought her back to the moment. She walked around her living room, admiring the turquoise accent wall adorned with varying colors of burnt orange wall art, small straw baskets, and an African mask. Gone are the days of monochromatic colors. It all looked strange and out of place, yet somehow, it all belonged together.

"Mom," Tianna called. "My friend is coming to dinner too, and since he drives, he offered to pick us up.

“Let’s take a walk before we meet him; it’s nice out.” Tianna was feeling a bit claustrophobic and Gregory was such an outdoorsman, so most of their dates involved walking, picnics, and other outdoor activities.

“I see a change in you,” her mother remarked as the warm, balmy air blew her now gray strands around. “What is it? Who is it?”

“Well, I have been seeing someone. It hasn’t been going on for an exceptionally long time, just a few months, so I didn’t tell you about it. I wanted to be sure I wasn’t wasting my time.”

“Well, there is nothing wrong with dating before jumping headfirst into anything. Getting to know a person takes time.”

“How’s Dad?”

“He is fine. He is his usual terrible self,” Lillian said with a hint of sarcasm. Her husband was back to his late-night escapades. Women, pool hall, liquor store, and horses. He’s moving slower these days, but he’s still at it.

“So, tell me about your mystery man.”

“Mom, you already *know* him; it’s Gregory.”

“Gregory? Who lives in Brock?” Lillian gestured vaguely with her thumb.

“Well. Yeah he moved here to New York a few years ago. He’s a radio personality; his sexy voice got him the job,” Tianna said as she secretly smiled to herself. When he held her close and put that voice on, it was close to heaven.

“Oh. Okay,” Lillian said, her face revealing her skepticism. She couldn't help but wonder why her daughter, who held a Ph.D., would date a radio disc jockey. What could they possibly have in common? As for dinner they went to Sylvia’s.

Meanwhile, Tianna’s days were taking on a new brightness, infused with the kind of excitement that made even ordinary moments feel significant. The days were becoming less mundane. When Gregory wasn’t around, the hours felt unbearably long. She enjoyed her job, but having someone to confide in made life richer. It felt good to think about someone who thought about her too. One afternoon, returning from lunch, Tianna found a stunning bouquet on her secretary’s desk.

“Look at you, Miss Mallory! Those are beautiful flowers.”

“Dr. McQueen, these are for you.”

“For me?” Tianna blinked, caught off guard. It wasn’t her birthday or any special occasion. The small card simply read, "I’m thinking of you. G." Tianna grinned like a schoolgirl. Maxine, her co-worker, hovered nearby, watching with narrowed eyes. Maxine slithered out of her office and headed to the receptionist desk. Eying the bouquet quickly commented.

“These flowers are pretty, but the petals are wilting already,” Maxine remarked, her tone dripping with disdain. Tianna rolled her eyes and mouthed, "JEALOUS," Mallory shook her head in agreement.

“You might want to add some water to those,” Maxine turned to walk to her office with a small smirk on her face. Mallory chimed in, “You ever receive flowers? Tianna laughed, feeling lighthearted and unbothered. Maxine’s negativity was becoming a joke in the office, and others began to notice her sour attitude.

“Uhhh, Maxine,” Mallory called out, stopping her in her tracks.

“Yes, Mallory?”

“Your skin looks fantastic! Have you been out in the sun? You know vitamin D is excellent for the body and for keeping the blues away.”

Maxine hesitated before replying, “Thank you,” unsure whether to accept the compliment or not. Finally, a small smile broke through. “Have a good day, too.” And walked back into her office, claiming that her allergies were acting up.

"She's so bitter and jealous," Mallory muttered once Maxine walked away. "I don't know anyone who needs vitamin D more. It could change her whole mood."

Anna from accounting piped in, "I know that's right! She's downright miserable, anyway."

"Please give me five minutes and take messages. I need to make a call, thanks Mallory," Tianna rushed off to call Gregory, eager to thank him for his thoughtful gesture.

Tianna took Northern trails train Brockton to see her father. When she arrived at the house, she immediately felt the emptiness. The air was thick with a silence that clung to the walls like an unwelcome guest. She called out, but there was no answer. She checked her phone—there was a message. Her father had been admitted to the hospital. A pang of anxiety settled in her chest, but she pushed it down, grabbed her keys, and headed straight for CuralHealth.

It was Wednesday, her requested day off, and the midweek lull gave the hospital an unusual stillness. As Tianna entered the building, she immediately noticed how clean the wood floors were, gleaming under the harsh fluorescent lights. The sharp scent of lemon cleaning products filled her nose, mingling with an underlying mustiness that seemed to seep from the walls. Every corner of the hospital sparkled, meticulously scrubbed, as if to distract from the underlying sorrow that pervaded its halls.

She made her way to see her father,, but as she passed each doorway, her thoughts drifted to Richie. His room—the room that had once been her sanctuary of memories—was now empty. She had finally cleared out all of his belongings, a task she had put off for so long. But even though the room was clean, the bed remained untouched, standing like a haunting reminder of what she had lost.

Had getting rid of Richie's things made the pain any easier? Tianna knew the answer was no. The emptiness didn't erase the memories; it only sharpened the edges of her regret. Clearing out the room was just another attempt at healing that fell short, another reminder that grief wasn't something you could pack away in boxes and push into a corner.

As she neared her father's room, she braced herself for the flood of emotions she knew would come. Her father had become a distant figure over the years, but seeing him in the hospital brought everything back—the resentment, the unspoken words, and the fragile hope that maybe, this time, things could be different.

Initially worried when she received her father's call, Tianna felt anger bubbling up through her relief. *Why*, Dad? she kept thinking. Why is drinking that important? The question had lingered in her mind for years, and now that she had a semblance of peace, she wondered why he wanted to talk to her.

As she walked to the hospital, she was intercepted by Dr. Moore, her father's attending physician, who looked worn-out after an all-nighter.

"Ms. McQueen, I presume, you're Ralph McQueen's family?"

"Umm, yes, I'm his daughter."

"Your mother came yesterday; she informed the staff that you'd be coming to visit." Dr. Moore straightened his glasses and white coat. "He mentioned he wouldn't go to AA, but I hoped you might convince him. Right now he was admitted for dehydration. Your father is receiving an IV drip right now."

The doctor continued on, "My fear is that your father's gap in memory will progress due to alcohol abuse. Hepatic Encephalopathy, I believe you are aware. But now because of that he has Hepatomegaly. It happens when the liver is so enlarged and damaged that it can no longer filter toxins from the blood. It could mean dialysis. Your father, if he does not stop drinking, the toxins will affect his brain function. Which can result in mild confusion or worse coma." The news was jarring, she did not know what to say. Tianna walked slowly to her father's room.

"Bravery," she whispered to herself as she approached Room 221. She entered, knowing the staff would be listening in, and helped her father into a wheelchair, taking him down the quiet hall.

"Tianna, baby, I'm glad you came to see your old man."

"Dad, you asked me to come."

"Yup," he said, then fell silent. "I want to talk to you."

"Okay, but first, Dad, I want to talk to you."

"No, I want to go first. It's important, and I want to say it before I lose my nerve."

Tianna sat back, hoping this was the moment he would finally admit he needed help. She watched him twist a napkin nervously in his hands, waiting for his revelation.

"You know," he began, "I was such a baby boy when I married your mother. My mother spoiled me rotten, and maturity wasn't my strength."

Tianna listened intently, her heart pounding. "Your mother was a prize for me. She was kind and pretty; I didn't know how to accept it. Her love was freely given, though I didn't deserve it." His eyes remained fixed on his lap.

"Dad, it's alright; we are here for you." Tianna placed her warm hand over his cold one. She knew what he wanted to tell her and did not want a sick man crying over something no one could change.

"You don't need to talk about this."

He looked up at her, tears brimming in his eyes.

"Richie's death….It was….. was avoidable."

"I know, Dad," she said gently. "That's all in the past now."

"What?" Tianna asked, her voice tight with disbelief.

"Mom confessed after Janiyah got drunk and spilled everything,"

"That damn girl and her mouth," he muttered, shaking his head. "How can this be your mama's fault, baby? I was supposed to be home, watching you two. I was selfish. Your mother was working that day, and all I had to do was keep you both safe. And how the hell did Janiyah even know?" He was working himself up, and Tianna reached over to calm him.

"Dad, Janiyah only repeated what she heard her parents gossiping about," she explained softly.

He exhaled sharply, his anger giving way to guilt. "If this is about the affair, your mom already told me. I didn't handle it right."

"Dad, Mom told me about it, too. She told me two months ago. And she also admitted she went out looking for you that night."

"She did?" he asked, his eyes narrowing with disbelief.

Tianna nodded, her heart heavy. "She told me she saw Richie that night. Told him to go back to bed. But instead…she snuck out. Richie woke up looking for both of you, and that's how he ended up getting hit by the car."

Her father sat back, his face a mix of sorrow and regret. Before Tianna could say more, her phone buzzed, breaking the moment. She considered ignoring it but realized her father needed rest. She gave him a reassuring pat on the hand before stepping out.

On the drive back, Tianna's thoughts drifted to her parents' complicated relationship. If there was a definition for a "marriage situationship," they were living it. Her reverie was interrupted by a call from Mallory, finalizing details for an upcoming conference in Arizona. Tianna wasn't thrilled about the trip but thought she might convince Gregory to come along. Sedona was beautiful in the fall—or any season, really.

The weekend trip home reminded Tianna of her college breaks. Back then, coming home was about decompressing—organizing, cleaning, and trying to reset and walking on eggshells around her mother.

At her own apartment, she did just that, straightening up before settling into her thoughts. Another call came, this time from Gregory. His warm voice lifted her spirits, inspiring her to do something she hadn't done before: cook a full meal for her mother.

"How was your day?" Tianna asked her mother later, surprising both of them.

"Fine," Lillian replied, a small smile breaking through her usual guarded demeanor. "Are you hungry?"

"Mom, why don't you sit down? Let me cook," Tianna said, surprising herself even more. It wasn't just about taking control—it was about seeing her mother relaxed, something Tianna hadn't fully appreciated before.

"Okay," Lillian said, eyeing her daughter curiously as she sat down.

Tianna prepared spaghetti with a red wine pasta sauce, using a recipe she had looked up earlier. Lillian was impressed and, for the first time in a long while, they laughed together like friends rather than mother and daughter. Over glasses of wine, Tianna shared funny stories from work, including a patient with obsessive-compulsive disorder who insisted she comfort his cat in bizarre ways.

"I see you smiling more often," Lillian said, a glimmer of hope softening her expression.

"I guess," Tianna replied with a shrug.

Later, as Tianna settled onto the sofa, cradling a glass of wine, her father's earlier question echoed in her mind. *Are you seeing anyone?*

She had told him about Gregory. "Maybe," she had said. "We've never talked about being exclusive, but we spend most of our free time together. I don't want to jinx it—it's been going strong for seven months."

"Darlin', you gotta speak up. Talk to him. Tell him how you feel," her father had advised, his voice steady even as he lay hooked up to the IV.

Now, Tianna thought about her father's words. Maybe she would talk to Gregory. After all, she felt better after speaking with her father—and she had a feeling he would be fine, too, with time.

Chapter EIGHTEEN

Marriage was never of Tianna's mind and she never broached the subject at all. Growing up, Tianna had always been wary of marriage. Watching her parents' debacle of a relationship made her believe that love came with pain, compromise, and emotional turmoil. She vowed never to settle for anything less than true partnership. Gregory, however, changed her perspective over time. His gentle nature and the way he treated his mother with such tenderness and respect softened her heart. He was considerate, thoughtful, and never made her feel like love was a battlefield to be won, but rather a place of mutual care and concern.

The idea of marriage was so low on her list of priorities when Gregory proposed, Tianna was momentarily overwhelmed, not by fear, but by the realization that she had found someone different—someone who made her feel safe and cherished. And she did not want to ruin it with marriage. But when he asked and then promised to be the husband she needed, he presented her with a stunning 2-carat pear-shaped ring, flanked by two small round sapphires on each side, each .25 carats. Oddly enough, it was the exact ring she had always imagined wearing, though she had never voiced this to anyone. It felt like fate, a sign that everything was aligning just as it should. So she said yes.

They celebrated the engagement with a small, intimate dinner, just their mothers in attendance. Both women were delighted, sharing stories and laughter over the meal. Tianna's heart felt full. Not needing anything at that moment. However, there was one absence that weighed heavily on her mind—her father, Ralph, could not join them. He was admitted again in the hospital, hooked up to IVs and heart monitoring tubes as doctors ran tests to figure out why he had been experiencing dizzy spells. Though his absence was felt, Tianna tried to stay positive, hoping for good news soon.

In that moment, despite the uncertainties of life, Tianna realized she was ready to embrace this next chapter with Gregory, knowing that she had found a love that didn't echo her parents' struggles but stood on its own foundation of respect, compassion, and trust. She wanted to see where their journey would end. It was a chance but somehow, she was willing to take it.

While away from her hometown and while working on other local cases. Detective Garcia had received a tip, something he hadn't expected after more than fifteen years. The hit-and-run case had long since gone cold, but he had never forgotten his promise to Lillian and her daughter, Tianna. The promise had weighed heavily on him over the years, not just because it was a personal commitment, but because of the raw grief he had seen in their eyes the day it happened. It was a grief he couldn't shake, one that had kept him coming back to the case, even when it seemed hopeless.

As he sat in his cluttered office, the familiar smell of stale coffee and the soft hum of the overhead lights surrounded him, evoking memories of countless nights spent poring over old files. The walls were adorned with case notes, photographs, and maps—reminders of battles fought against time and indifference. Garcia could still picture the scene: the sound of sirens piercing the quiet neighborhood, the frantic calls for help, and the helplessness that enveloped him as he tried to piece together the fragments of that fateful day.

This new lead felt like a flicker of light in the darkness. He had learned to approach tips with caution, each one a potential mirage in a desert of despair, but something about this one felt different. It wasn't just a whisper in the wind; it was grounded in specifics, names and places that danced tantalizingly at the edge of his memory. Could it be? He had chased so many false leads over the years that the thought of this one bearing fruit filled him with a mix of hope and skepticism.

The detective reached for the old case file, the edges worn and frayed from years of handling. As he flipped through the pages, he could feel the weight of the unsolved crime bearing down on him once more. Every detail mattered; every lead could be the one that brought justice. He was ready to dive back into the investigation, fueled by the faces of Lillian and Tianna—two women whose lives had been irrevocably changed. With renewed determination, he grabbed his coat and headed out the door, ready to follow this lead wherever it might take him.

The memory of that night still haunted him. A child, barely six years old, had wandered out into the street in the early morning hours after his mother had taken out the garbage. The driver, a drunk, had struck him and sped away. The boy never had a chance. Witnesses were scarce, and leads even scarcer. All Garcia had to go on was a vague description: a dark gray Chevrolet with tinted windows. The only solid piece of evidence was the personalized plate:

"215 AHOY." That had always been his best lead, but despite numerous database searches, the car seemed to vanish into thin air.

Now, all these years later, one of his sources called with new information. Garcia had learned not to get his hopes up too high after all this time, but something about this felt different. His source mentioned a car matching the description—same color, same model, same plate—recently resurfacing in a nearby town. It wasn't much, but it was more than he'd had in years. It was enough to reignite the fire inside him.

As he stood in his cluttered office, the dim light casting long shadows, Garcia looked at the photos pinned to the wall. The dead boy's face, frozen in time, stared back at him. Detective Lee dragged Richie's eyelids down. Beside it was a photo of Lillian, tear-streaked and broken. Tianna had been just eleven, but even her youthful face had carried the weight of the tragedy. Over the years, Garcia had kept in touch with them, particularly Lillian. She had become like family in a way. He had watched as she tried to piece her life back together, but he knew a part of her had died the night she lost her son.

And Tianna—well, she had grown up to be a strong, independent woman. She had thrown herself into her work, into her relationship with Gregory, and somewhere along the way, the case had drifted out of her life. But not for Lillian. Not for her husband, Ralph.

Garcia sat down at his desk, his fingers tapping rhythmically on the keyboard as he logged into the police database. His mind raced as he entered the details of the tip. If the plate was personalized, it would make narrowing down the search easier. It was just a matter of time before he found a match. He could almost feel it, the breakthrough he had been waiting for all these years.

The phone rang, startling him out of his thoughts. It was his sergeant, reminding him that they had other cases to solve. Garcia knew that, but the hit-and-run had always been his priority. He had promised his sergeant they'd solve it before the year was out. The timing couldn't have been more personal—Lee was set to retire next year, and this case had become his legacy, the one thing he wanted to close before hanging up his badge for good.

"I'm working on it," he reassured his sergeant, though the weight of the deadline pressed down on him.

After hanging up, Garcia leaned back in his chair, rubbing his temples. He knew time was running out, but something about this lead gave him hope. Maybe, just maybe, they would find the driver and finally bring closure to Lillian and Tianna.

Meanwhile, Tianna was blissfully unaware of the developments in the case. She had buried herself in her work and her relationship with Gregory. The case had become a distant memory, a painful chapter she had tried to close. She had enough on her plate—managing her career, juggling the complexities of her relationship, and navigating life as an adult. The case was something her mother clung to, but Tianna had long since distanced herself from it. Cases over two years were harder to solve or get a conviction.

Garcia, on the other hand, didn't have time to dwell on the emotional intricacies. He had a job to do. The lead he had received seemed promising, but there were still so many unknowns. Would the car lead him to the driver? Was the driver still even alive, or had they lived these fifteen years without a second thought about the life they had taken?

He closed his eyes for a moment, taking a deep breath. He had solved countless cases in his career, but none felt as personal as this one. He knew the emotional toll it had taken on Lillian, and by extension, Tianna. And for him, it wasn't just another case—it was a promise, one he intended to keep, no matter how long it took.

The screen in front of him blinked as the NDR database search finally returned a result. "So…., He was on the National Driver Registry." Garcia's eyes widened as he read the report. The car—dark gray 1986 Chevrolet, tinted windows, plate 215 AHOY—had been flagged just last week. It had been impounded in a nearby town for unpaid parking violations.

He grabbed his jacket and keys, his pulse quickening. This was it. After all these years, he might finally have the answer. One step closer to fulfilling his promise to Lillian and bringing justice to her son. He dialed Lillian's number, knowing the conversation they were about to have would change everything.

When Tianna received the call she dreaded, it was the third week of April, but instinctively knew it was inevitable. Her father, who had started discussing going to an AA meeting, could not resist the urge to drink. It beckoned him as he walked to speak with his wife about attending AA. That day, he fought a losing battle. On his way to the pool hall, his friend Billy offered him a drink, and to be polite, he accepted. Ralph was still haunted by Richie's memory, born in early May, and he felt responsible for his son's death, believing he had urged him to drink excessively.

Both men were expelled from the pool hall for drunkenness and rowdiness. "And don't come back, Ralph. Always startin' sum mess," the bartender yelled. Clinton staggered in the direction of his home. Ralph staggered to a nearby liquor store, bought more alcohol, and the n attempted to return home. Since leaving rehab. He promised to stop drinking, but every time he thought about Lillian and Richie he couldn't. When his legs betrayed him. He faltered causing him to collapse while crossing the street. Bill, a part-time store clerk propped up against the local grocery store, did not help. “Drunkies,” was the only word he uttered and walked back inside. Ralph erected himself barely standing in the street, swaying as cars honked and swerved to avoid hitting him. He tried to challenge them with slurred, unintelligible threats, his only response being a middle finger to passing vehicles.

Ralph’s headache started at the back of his head and travelled towards the front down his face causing his jaw to throb as well. Shards of pain were pounding, an unrelenting pressure that refused to let up. He felt nauseous. The stomach swam and his head thundered.

Each step he took felt heavier than the last, his vision blurring as the pain spread across his forehead and down his neck. He eventually made it across the street safely, but the agony only intensified. The bright lights from passing cars and traffic signals seemed to warp and blur, creating a dizzying kaleidoscope that made him stumble. His heart raced as his breath grew shallow.

At 11:01 PM on a Friday night, Ralph died from a stroke. His body collapsed on the sidewalk, but the ambulance was delayed. Those who passed by assumed he was merely another drunk sleeping off the night’s excesses. They never imagined that within him, his life was slowly slipping away. In his final moments, he was haunted by his wife’s warnings about his health, his daughter’s encouraging words, and his doctor's grim predictions that seemed to echo louder than ever. It was piercing.

The last image in his mind was Richie's face, the memory fading into the darkness as strangers gathered around. Some people muttered, "I know that guy—he's always drunk. Let him sleep it off." A group of teenagers rifled through his pockets, searching for anything of value. Others simply shook their heads and moved on, urging their friends to leave the "drunk bum alone." By the time help arrived, it was too late.

Another passing teen kicked at Ralph's foot, getting no response. He kicked harder, prompting another boy to declare, "Yo, Mickey, stop kicking him; the dude is dead."

"How do *you* know? He is just a drunk bum."

An older man, overhearing this, asked, "Will you continue kicking a dead man or call an ambulance?" Shaking his head at their genius, he walked away.

"I was just about to do that," the boy yelled, now feeling squeamish for interacting with a deceased body. Ralph was pronounced dead on arrival at the hospital.

Lillian received the call after one in the morning. She cried, poured a glass of his favorite drink, spent an hour at home, she expected this, just not this way. Lillian identified her husband at the morgue. This was very ironic, she thought. "Tianna will be devastated," she thought. He had seemed to be making progress, and she had hoped he would change to live longer. Staring at the sheet covering her husband's face, the room reeked of a bar. Lillian collected his belongings, took a deep breath, and decided to call Tianna the day after tomorrow to give herself time to cope.

However, battling with herself to wait longer, she broke down and called her daughter at ten on the following Saturday. When a sober Lillian arrived, her daughter knew then that her father died. Gregory called that very moment.

Tianna's scream pierced the line when Gregory answered. Tianna expected her fathers death but it hurt nonetheless. He rushed over to see her, comfort her. He listened and held the distraught Tianna as she struggled to breathe. Gregory, always the gentleman, fetched a glass of water, wiped her tears, and cradled her in his arms. The days that followed were a blur as arrangements were made. Ralph's favorite colors, navy blue and burgundy, were incorporated into the funeral leaflets, and a navy suit was chosen for him. Lillian put aside her negative feelings and managed everything, prompting Tianna to recognize her mother's dedication and sacrifices.

Tianna, devastated by her father's actions, felt immense disappointment. The hero she had admired was not the man she thought he was. The realization of his hypocrisy, his struggles with alcohol, and his treatment of her mother were crushing. Tianna discovered her father had blamed her mother for his failures and infidelities, including a miscarriage that never happened. It became clear that Richie's death was another way Ralph manipulated Lillian with guilt. Tianna saw how her mother had endured so much, working tirelessly every day despite her own suffering. For the first time, Tianna understood the trauma bonding her mother endured, despite her professional knowledge of it.

Across town at that same moment the database that Det. Garcia used, yielded something. Personalized plates were common however the make and color of the car along with the plate held him up until. He took a trip to the PBA office about a police corruption case. He spotted someone with a familiar face wearing Dockers white shirt with a pocket protector that held wire rimmed glasses, it was Victor.

Tianna had remained her father's favorite until the end. Ralph's mistress had a son, Robert Richard McQueen, whom Lillian took surprisingly well. At sixty-three, Ralph's death and his lover's age of forty-two seemed absurd. Lillian humorously speculated about the baby's paternity, pondering if Ralph had bought Viagra and condoms at the Dollar store. Before the funeral, the child's mother inquired about social security benefits. Some would argue about her paying the life insurance policy for her husband but it came in handy. After the funeral and giving his daughter some money, then paying off the second mortgage, with minimal funds remaining, Lillian provided fifteen thousand for the baby from the life insurance and planned a trip to Merida, Spain. She had never traveled internationally and was excited for the adventure. And of course the clerk, Merida from her old job, was welcomed to come if her husband allowed it.

As rain gently tapped against the limousine window on the day of Ralph's funeral, Tianna tried not to not cry unless reminded of her father's words. Only she and her mother remained, and their relationship felt less fragile. They needed one another. On the day of the repast it was standing room only in the small living room. The women gathered in the kitchen. Lillian, complaining about her hair, was consoled by the neighborhood's support. Plates of food, including Agatha's famous lasagna, came and went. Mr. Baker, despite his strained relationship with Ralph, showed up, and the event transitioned from somber church music to Ralph's favorite raunchy soul tunes.

By evening, Lillian was relieved when her brother-in-law left early. She chose not to disclose Ralph's child or its mother to avoid additional stress. She focused on maintaining peace and honoring her husband's memory, grateful for Gregory's support and reassured by the continued presence of her community. The days drifted by after the funeral, each one blending into the next like colors in a watercolor painting. Lillian soon found herself planning her return to Florida, a bittersweet prospect. Happy to return to a tranquil place where she created new memories but not happy to leave her daughter behind.

She had offered Tianna the house, a gesture laden with love, but Tianna declined, preferring to stay close to her job and avoid the solitude of the old place. As Lillian began the daunting task of cleaning up, she stumbled upon various old items hidden in the corners of rooms, some evoking fond memories of laughter and warmth, while others stirred less pleasant emotions of loss and regret.

Among the relics was a small box containing a gift from Ralph from their dating years, a simple token of his affection that now felt heavy with significance. Nestled inside was a letter, ink faded yet still legible, written just months before his death. Lillian had barely touched the things from the house since then, each item a reminder of what she had lost. Sitting on her old paisley couch, surrounded by the ghosts of the past, she carefully opened the letter addressed simply to 'Lillian.' As she read, a flood of emotions washed over her—nostalgia, sorrow, and a glimmer of the love they once shared, all swirling together like the dust dancing in the fading light. However it was the note that left more confusing emotions than she could put words to, at least he remembered her in the end.

Dearest Lillian,

I hope that you read this after I have gone. I am sorry I did not know how to love anyone; I spent the years with you selfishly chasing every imagined youthful thing I could. I never meant to hurt you, Tianna, or Richie. It was never your fault. I take responsibility; I know it is too late. You were the blessing that was given to me. I was afraid to love you too much, so instead, I hurt you. Again, I am sorry, I did not deserve you. I always loved you and only you.

Love always,

Ralph

Lillian stared at the note, struck by the openness, a stark contrast to the indifference she had felt from Ralph in recent years. "He must have written this on a lucid day," she murmured, struggling to understand why these words had come so late. It was bittersweet, offering no real closure. Ralph was gone, unable to face her and say everything she needed to hear. It felt like too little, too late. She slowly reread the note, placed it in her suitcase, wrapped the wooden jewelry box, and packed it away. His last words were significant but incomplete; the guilt over their son's passing still gnawed at her. Lillian's gaze drifted across the worn, familiar room. A bittersweet nostalgia washed over her as she thought of her late husband. The old house, once a symbol of love and family, now felt like a decaying relic.

Its peeling paint and creaky floorboards mirrored the passage of time. The task of sorting through her husband's and son's belongings was a painful reminder of their absence. Each item, a fragment of their lives, evoked a mix of sorrow and cherished memories.

The house, with its outdated electrical work and leaky plumbing, was a constant source of worry. The thought of expensive repairs and the daunting prospect of maintaining such an old property overwhelmed her. She considered renting it out, but the necessary renovations seemed insurmountable. The weight of the house, both physical and emotional, was becoming too much to bear.

Staying in the old house felt like waiting for an inevitable disaster. Something was always either leaking or in need of repairs. The task of sorting through her husband's and son's belongings was emotionally draining. The house, with its peeling paint, creaky floorboards, and outdated electrical work, was more a burden than a comfort. She considered renting it out but realized it would require extensive repairs she couldn't afford. The thought of it all made her head spin.

Two weeks later Detective Garcia had received a tip, something he hadn't expected after more than fifteen years. The hit-and-run case had long since gone cold, but he had never forgotten his promise to Lillian and her daughter, Tianna. The promise had weighed heavily on him over the years, not just because it was a personal commitment, but because of the raw grief he had seen in their eyes the day it happened. It was a grief he couldn't shake, one that had kept him coming back to the case, even when it seemed hopeless.

Garcia reached for the old case file, the edges worn and frayed from years of handling. As he flipped through the pages, he could feel the weight of the unsolved crime bearing down on him once more. Every detail mattered; every lead could be the one that brought justice. He was ready to dive back into the investigation, fueled by the faces of Lillian and Tianna—two women whose lives had been irrevocably changed. With renewed determination, he grabbed his coat and headed out the door, ready to follow this lead wherever it might take him. It was months later but the NDR was the key.

Finding a quiet corner in the living room, Lillian unfolded the coffee-stained letter and broke into a cry that was both pitiful and cathartic. It wasn't a cleansing release but rather an outpouring of grief over the lateness of Ralph's words. Later that year Detective Garcia stood in the courtroom, watching as Victor Gordon faced sentencing.

Years ago, Victor had been arrested for driving drunk, which had cost him his job and reputation. On the night of the accident, he had once again been drinking, taking a wrong turn into a quiet cul-de-sac in a neighborhood he wasn't familiar with. The tragic hit-and-run that followed had left a family shattered.

Despite his age—sixty—Victor had become a respected figure in his community, even serving the local Police Benevolent Association (PBA), a position that reflected his deep ties to law enforcement. The predominantly Irish-American police force, of which members of Victor's family were a huge part, had weighed his long-standing service in their assessment. Nonetheless, the court charged him with vehicular manslaughter, and he was sentenced to five years in prison. However, considering his age, remorse, the judge reduced his sentence to six months.

Lillian, the mother of the victim, sat quietly beside her daughter Tianna, holding hands. She played with the small handkerchief in her hand. Victor was led away. She had decided long before that day to read a letter of forgiveness, acknowledging her role in the circumstances leading to her son's death. Victor had apologized to both Lillian and Tianna, expressing genuine sorrow for the pain he caused.

Though Lillian accepted his apology, she knew deep down that it was time to move on, not only from the tragedy but also from the guilt she had carried. As she stood up to leave, she felt a strange sense of peace wash over her. In that moment, she understood that forgiveness wasn't just for Victor—it was for her, too. The road ahead would still be difficult, but she was finally ready to take the first step toward healing.

The following month a retired Sergeant Lee entered the hall to thunderous applause and cheers for thirty-seven years of service. He wore dark blue, gold medals swinging like a pendulum from his suit. Fresh buzz cut and wearing a smile he could not hide. Nary a scandal attached to his name. And solving yet another case right before his retirement party was no small feet. He was one of a kind, he grudgingly mentioned Detective Garcia, without him, Lee would have not closed the case so Lee had no choice. Lillian and Tianna were invited to speak. They expressed their gratitude for Lees' and Detective Garcia's tenacity. Many other victims or family of victims spoke and Tianna was touched at how a dedicated officer did in fact change lives for the better.

It took some time and prayer but Lillian and her daughter Tianna had finally and successfully rebuilt their relationship through mutual respect and the honoring of boundaries, marked by honest conversations. Time had indeed healed many of their wounds, allowing them to move forward together.

Lillian's condo in Florida, near the beach, had become her dream home. She was close enough to hear the crashing waves and smell the Atlantic. If she closed her eyes, she could feel the misty spray rising from the water. Now, she was single and living alone— a widow with an adult, married child, and soon to be a grandmother. She envisioned peaceful morning walks along the shore and hoped Tianna would visit as often as she could. Tianna had married Gregory last year, just two years after her grandmother Gloria passed away. The vibrant community of Pensacola, with its large retirement population, stood in stark contrast to their former home in Brockton, and the pleasant weather suited Lillian perfectly.

While Lillian struggled to forgive her husband Ralph's imperfections, she was gradually learning to let go of her resentment and embrace the lessons that had come from their relationship. She realized that holding onto anger was a weight she no longer wanted to carry. Each day brought her closer to understanding the power of forgiveness—not just for Ralph, but for herself. It wasn't easy, and some days were harder than others, but Lillian was determined to focus on the future rather than the past.

Despite the distance that remained between Tianna and her mother, Lillian, she made a conscious effort to check in on her regularly, though not as often as Lillian might have hoped. Her daughter could have gone "No Contact." And Lillian would have not blamed her. Their relationship had its ups and downs, marked by years of misunderstanding and unspoken words, but it was also evolving into something more open and compassionate. Tianna's calls, though infrequent, were a reminder that she still cared, even if she expressed it in her own way.

Gregory, on the other hand, acted like another son Lillian was grateful, he called often to see how she was doing and making sure she felt valued and loved. His regular check-ins warmed Lillian's heart, filling a void that had been there for years. She was deeply grateful that Tianna had found someone like Gregory—a man who not only loved her daughter unconditionally but wasn't afraid to show it in the small, thoughtful gestures that truly mattered.

Tianna often teased Gregory about his habit of sending little gifts to her mother in Florida—small tokens that always seemed to arrive just when Lillian needed a reminder that she wasn't alone. And Tianna promised that once their lives settled down a bit, they'd visit Lillian with their grandbaby, creating new memories to cherish. Lillian couldn't help but smile at the thought of having them all together, her family finally finding a semblance of peace and happiness.

As their lives continued to intertwine, Lillian found herself cherishing every moment of this renewed bond, feeling a deep sense of joy watching Tianna step into a life filled with love and understanding. Gregory's presence had not only changed Tianna's world but had also brought healing to their fractured family. And for the first time in a long while, Lillian felt hope—a hope that the past could be left behind and that, in the end, love and forgiveness would lead them all to the peace they had long sought.

The End

The following are suggested discussion questions that dive into complex themes related to family dynamics, responsibility, and the challenges faced by the African American community.

These questions give an explanation and deep dive into the absence or infrequency of fathers in the home and community contribute to the rarity of African American nuclear families, and how does this impact the emotional and financial stability of those families?

1a) Do mothers in these families accept behaviors or circumstances they otherwise wouldn't because of the perceived scarcity of intact nuclear families, and how does this influence their decision-making?

1b) Why is Lillian always reflecting while doing household chores?

2) Is the protagonist, Tianna McQueen, in denial or unaware of her father's unemployment and struggles with alcohol addiction, and how does this affect her perception of him?

3) While Ralph had long struggled with alcohol, did the trauma of losing his son accelerate his downward spiral, or were there other factors at play?

4) Can Ralph be considered a responsible father simply because he remained physically present in the home, or does his emotional absence undermine his role as a parent?

5) Does Ralph hold any responsibility for Richie's death, either directly or indirectly, and how should this shape our understanding of his character?

6) Why did Lillian remain with her husband despite the challenges? Could it be attributed to Trauma Bonding?

7) Lillian did not confront her husband's behavior. Was this due to her adherence to traditional feminine roles? Despite being the sole provider, was she leading the household from a masculine position?

8) What aspirations does Lillian hold for her daughter? Professional or personal?

9) What lessons did Tianna glean from observing her parents' relationship?

10) Did the exercise work, to help repair the miscommunication between the two?

11) Is Tianna at risk of repeating her mother's relationship mistakes?

12) Does Tianna prefer her father over her mother, and if so, why?

13) Is the concept of the African American nuclear family becoming obsolete? If so, what are the contributing factors? Is Tianna compromising in her relationship with Gregory, or is she genuinely

comfortable and happy with him because of their shared cultural background?

The Comfortable Lie delves into the complexities of familial relationships, exploring themes of love, regret, and the long-lasting impacts of trauma. It examines the roles and expectations placed on family members, particularly within the African American community, and how these roles shape their identities and decisions.

Towards the end of the story Lillian prepares to return to Florida, the strain of her relationship with her daughter weighs heavily on her mind. She realizes that a parent should never take their bond with their children for granted—children, after all, have the right to sever ties. The lie she told about her son's death could have easily done just that. In an attempt to make amends, she offers Tianna the proceeds from selling the family home, but Tianna declines, preferring to stay close to her job and avoid the isolation that the old house represents.

Sorting through Richie and then later Ralph's belongings was a heart-wrenching task for Lillian, each item a painful reminder of the lives she had lost, stirring a flood of bittersweet memories that left her caught between sorrow and the quiet resolve to move forward. Amid her search, she stumbles upon a letter Ralph wrote months before his death. In it, he apologizes, confessing his regrets and acknowledging his shortcomings. Reading the letter, Lillian saw a side of Ralph she hadn't seen in years. In that moment, she felt a sense of closure.

www.ingramcontent.com/pod-product-compliance
Ingram Content Group UK Ltd.
Pitfield, Milton Keynes, MK11 3LW, UK
UKHW021911190726
13853UKWH00002B/616

9 798330 462568